Sally Ann Voak's

HOLIDAY

COUNTDOWN

DIET

Published by
Peter Grose Ltd
Monmouth

Printed and bound in Great Britain for Peter Grose Ltd by The
Bath Press, Bath, Avon.

British Library C.I.P.
A catalogue record for this book is available from the
British Library
ISBN: 1-898-88516-8

Holiday Countdown Diet

By the same author
The She *Book Of Beauty*
The She *Book Of Slimming*
Fit For Life (with Daley Thompson)
The Fatfield Diet
The Fatfield Recipe Book
100 New Diets
A New You In 30 Days

THE HOLIDAY COUNTDOWN DIET

Life's a beach...so slim down, shape up and enjoy it!

Travel can broaden the mind—and the waistline. It's therefore always a good idea to shed a few pounds (or even more, if you're already overweight) before you go away. We all like to look our carefree best in holiday clothes and there's nothing like being a lighter-weight you to put a smile on your face and a spring in your step as you head off.

This book will help you lose weight simply and safely so you look and feel your best, whether you've chosen a beach holiday, city sight-seeing, or two weeks of active sports or exploration.

These days, holidays come at many different times of the year and some of us are lucky enough to be able to take two or three breaks annually. There is not always a great deal of time to plan our wardrobes or launch into a pre-holiday body beautiful campaign. We no longer spend all winter dreaming about that annual two-week break in July. Our holiday patterns are very different now, with short breaks, both at home and abroad, being enjoyed by people of all income-levels. When the opportunity to take a break comes (even if it's because we've suddenly been made redundant) we grab it with both hands!

That's why I've given you a choice of NINE diet programmes which will cater for long, short—or very short—holiday countdown times. You can slim for two months, a month, two weeks or even just three days before jetting off. It's up to you.

All these diets are economical, with simple recipes and menus designed to help you save vital cash for your holiday.

Before you choose your diet, remember that exercise is vital too. Choose a programme that includes at least three 20-minute periods of aerobic exercise each week (e.g. step workout, jogging, swimming, cycling) plus body-shaping routines for problem areas.

You can use any of the diets to help you slim for other special occasions in your life as well: a wedding, anniversary, Christmas or a special party.

Do remember that it is always a good idea to check

with your doctor before trying this or any other diet plan.

And what about while you're away on holiday? You won't want to put all those pounds back on, so I've included a chapter which gives the calorie count for some of the most popular foods you'll find abroad.

When you get back, you'll want to keep that healthy shape. So you'll find a final chapter which tells you how to settle into a pattern of healthy eating back home which will keep you in trim while offering you plenty of great foods to enjoy.

So good luck. Travel light (I'm not talking about your luggage) and have many happy hols!

—Sally Ann Voak

FOOD MEASUREMENT AND RECIPE GUIDE

Y ou will find a recipe section at the end of most of the diets featured in this book. Where dishes listed in diets are marked with an asterisk (*), recipes for these will be found in the accompanying recipe section at the end of the chapter.

All recipe ingredients as well as food and drink quantities stipulated in this book are in imperial measures—that is, pounds, ounces and fluid ounces.

One ounce is equivalent to 28.4 grams and one fluid ounce is 28.4 millilitres. However, it is easier to calculate metric amounts by taking 25 grams as the equivalent of one ounce. If a recipe calls for two ounces of cheese, say, allow 50 grams.

Drinks are in pub measures—that is, 1/3 gill (50ml) for aperitifs and vermouths; 1/2 pint (284ml) for beers and lagers; 5fl oz (142ml) for wines and 1/6 gill (25ml) for spirits. If a diet demands "a small glass" of any liquid this means a wine glass (5fl oz).

Diets sometimes mention specific brands like Birds

Eye and Findus because these are available in most countries. I also refer to supermarkets' own-brand products, naming British chains like Tesco, Sainsbury and Safeway—which should cause no problems for non-British readers. Around the world calorie or kilojoule values for these products may vary slightly. Check the label.

All spoon measures are level spoonfuls. If you use heaped spoonfuls, the calorie count will go up.

One tablespoon (tbs) equals 15ml

One dessertspoon (dsp) equals 10ml

One teaspoon (tsp) equals 5ml.

Eggs are size 3 (medium) unless the recipe says otherwise.

Use freshly-ground pepper when the recipe asks for pepper.

Ovens should always be pre-heated to the specified temperature.

Sally's Slimming Tips

Make it snappy! Holiday pictures can be very revealing. If you've always avoided being photographed on the beach, this is the year to play it clever. Look your slimmest by: (1) standing three-quarters to the camera, holding in your tum and bum; (2) choosing a costume that really does flatter your figure—and having a sarong handy to whip over your wobbly bits!

Give yourself a goal—even if it's ambitious! Cut out a picture of your favourite supermodel, wearing a bikini. Stick it on your 'fridge with the snapshot of YOUR face on top of Naomi's beautiful mug, or Claudia's incredible visage. Now you know what you could look like with the right diet and exercise programme! Or, if that sounds like pie in the sky, simply dig out an old picture taken when you were slimmer and fitter.

Every time you're tempted to reach for a slice of cheesecake, gaze at the picture and drink a long, cool glass of water. You can do it!

EAT A LOT....AND SLIM YOUR BOT!

Y ou can eat AS MUCH AS YOU LIKE of the
following very low calorie vegetables on each
of the Holiday Countdown Diets. So pile them up
on your plate and tuck in without a single guilt pang.
  Just remember one important rule before you start:
it is vital to eat EVERYTHING listed in a day's diet,
even if you think you are not hungry at the time.
There are vitamins, nutrients and elements which all
of us need as part of our daily food intake in order to
remain healthy. The diets here have been designed
with that in mind.
  So here goes with your "free list" foods which can
be eaten in unlimited quantities each day and will do
you good without hindering weight loss.
  Asparagus, Beansprouts, Broccoli, Cabbage, Carrots, Cauliflower, Celery, Chicory, Cucumber, En-
dive, Gherkins, Leeks, Lettuce, Mushrooms, Mustard and Cress, Peppers (red and green), Radishes,

Runner Beans, Spinach, Spring Greens, Spring Onions, Tomatoes (canned or fresh), Watercress.

Seasoning: use black pepper, herbs, garlic and lemon juice freely. Go easy on the salt.

Drink as much tap water or mineral water as you like. Go a little bit easy on the diet soft drinks, not because they are fattening themselves but because they may give you a "sweet tooth". However, on most of the Countdown diets you can drink moderate amounts of unsweetened black tea or milkless coffee as you like, plus, in most cases, half a pint of skimmed milk to be consumed each day as you wish.

You will notice, as you study the recipes at the end of most of the diet plans, that butter, cream and oil play almost no part in them. This is because the way you cook food is most important if it is to be low in calories. Even free-list food like mushrooms will not do your waistline any good if they are smothered in a cream sauce or fried in a dollop of butter.

On the other hand, the supposedly fattening potato can be an excellent diet food as long as butter and cream are not used in its preparation and it is not fried in a bath of oil. A jacket baked potato filled with chives and low-fat yogurt is filling, delicious, high in fibre and diet-sensible.

On arrival at your holiday spot, check out local restaurants to find those with good, fresh meals. Not that you will want to be watching your waistline every time you eat out—but at the same time you probably won't want to pig out at every opportunity, having got yourself in such good shape beforehand.

It is amazing how you get a taste for piles of crunchy salad and simple grills when you find they keep you in trim. So if dishes at some of the local eateries are served swimming in grease, or smothered in sauce, avoid them as much as you can. If in doubt, stick to grilled fish and meat, lots of vegetables (no sauces or butter), fruits and bread.

Important: If you are going to a tropical or semi-tropical country or have doubts about local hygiene standards, it is vital to seek advice both before you go and locally. Consult your doctor and your travel company.

If you are advised that the local water is not safe for drinking, for instance, you would be wise to steer clear of salads which may have been washed in dodgy water—or not washed at all. If you're self-catering, of course, you can wash your fruit and veg in bottled water. And it goes without saying that the only water you should drink should be the bottled kind—even in tea and coffee. Beware, also, if you're offered ice with your gin and tonic: don't risk it unless you are 100 per cent certain it was made with bottled water.

The least recommended way to stay slim on holiday is through food poisoning, diarrhoea or worse. So do check the safety of the food and water at your destination before you go.

FOUR WEEKS ON FISH...
LOOK LIKE A DISH!

Jetting off for some sun, sea and sexy frolics in just four weeks? You can look sleek and shapely in your swim-suit with this great diet. It's based around fish—all kinds, from cod to kippers.

Combine your fishy diet with a daily 20-minute swim in your local pool and you'll be as streamlined as a mermaid by the time you hit that sundrenched foreign shore.

Fish is an excellent choice for slimmers because it is generally lower in calories than meat. For instance, a 6oz (150g) piece of cod, grilled with a little low-fat spread, contains about 200 calories. The same amount of steak, also grilled with a little low-fat spread, would add about 400 calories to your daily food allowance—a fact worth weighing up when shopping for slimline meals!

Fatty fish like trout and mackerel make excellent, satisfying meals for slimmers and are especially good for your health since they contain an abundance of essential fatty acids, which help beat heart disease. Also, because they are oily, these fish do not require any extra fat in cooking. A large trout, grilled, would only set you back about 250 calories. If you add just a large salad from your "free" list and a piece of fresh fruit for dessert, you can have a filling feast that tots up only 300 calories.

Beware, though, of fish which is canned in oil: this simply adds calories which you don't need. Instead, look for tuna canned in brine, sardines in brine or tomato sauce.

Fish also has the advantage of being extremely quick to cook, particularly if you have a microwave oven. And many of the ready-prepared fish dishes available from your local supermarket are absolutely delicious. In fact, many are good enough for a posh dinner party without the hassle of lengthy preparation.

This diet includes all kinds of fishy ideas. You can choose fresh, tinned, packet, or even cooked fish from the chippie! And we give you meat and cheese alternatives for the occasions when you want a change from seafood.

This programme allows you to consume a generous 1200 calories daily, including a few treats like occasional glasses of wine or spirit-plus-mixers to cheer you on your way.

Follow Weeks One and Two carefully, then repeat them for a further two weeks. You could lose up to a stone.

WEEK ONE

BREAKFASTS
Choose one each day from this list:

Sandwich of two slices bread, lettuce, tomato, 2oz (50g) tuna-in-brine.

Findus Lean Cuisine Fisherman's Pie, one crispbread with a little low-fat spread.

One slice toast topped with small can (Heinz 5.3oz, 110g) baked beans, grilled tomatoes, one orange.

One quarter-pint (142ml) unsweetened fruit juice, 1oz (25g) any unsweetened cereal, milk from allowance, one apple or pear.

One slice toast topped with one small can John West pilchards or Smoked Tuna, canned in brine.

One slice toast, one size 3 egg, poached or boiled, one crispbread with a little low-fat spread and 1 tsp jam or honey.

MONDAY

Lunch: 3-1/2oz (100g) can pink salmon or tuna, salad from "free" list with lemon juice dressing, one crispbread with a little low-fat spread, one pear.

Supper: 6oz (150g) smoked haddock poached in water, small can (Heinz 205g) spaghetti in tomato sauce topped with 1/2 oz (12g) grated Edam cheese, green vegetables from "free" list, one small banana.

TUESDAY

Lunch: Sandwich of two slices bread with salad from "free" list and 1oz (25g) lean ham OR one pot Shippams Anchovy, Bloater or Crab paste.

Supper: Birds Eye Cod in Parsley or Cheese Sauce OR Menu Master Chicken and Mushroom Casserole OR Liver with Onions and Gravy, one 7oz (175g) jacket potato, vegetables from "free" list, one Ross frozen mousse OR 1oz (25g) vanilla ice cream.

WEDNESDAY

Lunch: One mug Batchelor's Slim-a-Soup, any flavour, one crispy roll with salad filling and 1oz (25g) grated Edam cheese, one orange.

Supper: Baked Fish with Butter Beans* OR one 10oz (250g) chicken portion, grilled or roast (no skin) with 3oz (75g) McCain oven chips PLUS salad and/or vegetables from "free" list.

THURSDAY

Lunch: One sandwich of two slices bread with salad from "free" list and two mashed pilchards canned in tomato sauce, with lemon juice.

Supper: One large slice melon, Fish Plaki* or one 5oz (125g) lean lamb chop with thin gravy, one 7oz (175g) jacket potato, salad from "free" list, one apple.

FRIDAY

Lunch: 4oz (100g) prawns, salad from "free" list, one crispy roll with a little low-fat spread and 1oz (25g) Edam cheese.

Supper: One portion cod-in-batter from chip shop, sachet of ketchup, half portion chips, salad from "free" list OR 5oz (125g) lean rump steak, 7oz (175g) jacket potato, salad and vegetables from "free" list, 1oz (25g) vanilla icecream.

SATURDAY

Lunch: Two slices toast topped either with one size 3 egg, poached, and grilled tomatoes OR one can John West Mackerel Fillets in Tomato Sauce.

Supper: One Birds Eye or Waitrose French Bread Pizza, any flavour, 3oz (75g) McCain oven chips, salad from "free" list, a few grapes.

SUNDAY

Lunch: 3oz (75g) any lean, roast meat with thin gravy OR casserole of 6oz (150g) white fish cooked with low-calorie mushroom soup, onions, tomatoes, herbs, 2oz (50g) roast or 5oz (125g) jacket potato, vegetables from "free" list, 2oz (50g) peas, two slices pineapple, fresh or canned in juice, 1 tbs (15ml) natural, low-fat yogurt.

Supper: One slice toast topped with one grilled fish cake, 1 tbs (15ml) tomato sauce, salad from "free" list, one banana.

WEEK TWO

BREAKFASTS

Choose one each day from this list:

1oz (25g) any unsweetened cereal, one slice toast with 1 tsp (5ml) jam or marmalade, one apple.

4oz (100g) grilled kipper with lemon juice and two crispbreads with a little low-fat spread.

4oz (100g) herring roes fried in 1/2oz (12g) low-fat spread on one slice toast

One size 3 poached or boiled egg, one slice toast with a little low-fat spread, one apple

Two grilled fish cakes, canned tomatoes, two crispbreads with a little low-fat spread.

MONDAY

Lunch: 4oz (100g) carton Shape cottage cheese, one crusty roll with salad from "free" list, one banana.

Supper: 1/2 grapefruit, Fish Creole*, salad from "free" list.

TUESDAY

Lunch: One sandwich of two slices bread, 4oz (100g) prawns, 1 tbs low-calorie seafood dressing, one apple.

Supper: One Birds Eye Cod Fish Cake in Crisp Crunch Crumb, 2oz (50g) peas, 3oz (75g) McCain oven chips, 3oz (75g) sweetcorn, salad and/or vegetables from "free" list, a few grapes.

WEDNESDAY

Lunch: One mug Batchelor's Slim a Soup, any flavour, one crusty roll with salad from "free" list, 1oz (25g) grated Edam cheese, one banana.

Supper: One serve St. Michael Fruits de Mer or Haddock and Cauliflower Cheese OR two well-grilled beefburgers, grilled tomatoes and 2oz (50g) sweetcorn PLUS 3oz (75g) mashed potato (use skimmed milk for mashing), salad from "free" list.

THURSDAY

Lunch: One scotch egg with salad from "free" list OR one sandwich of two slices bread with salad from "free" list plus one 3-1/2 oz (100g) can tuna-in-brine.

Supper: 6oz (150g) any oily fish (herring, mackerel, trout) stuffed with 1oz (25g) breadcrumbs, grated lemon rind, lemon juice, and 1/4 oz (7g) low-fat spread then baked in moderate oven (180°C, 350°F, Gas Mark 4) about 20 minutes. Serve with vegetables and salad from "free" list, 1oz (25g) ice cream with one slice pineapple, fresh or canned in juice.

FRIDAY

Lunch: One can Batchelors Farmhouse Vegetable Soup, two crispbreads with a little low-fat spread, a few grapes.

Supper: One portion haddock fried in batter from fish and chip shop, half portion chips, salad from "free" list OR 3oz (75g) (dry weight) pasta topped with sauce made from canned tomatoes, herbs, garlic, 4oz (100g) prawns or clams, one crispy roll PLUS salad from "free" list.

SATURDAY

Lunch: One slice toast topped with small can (Heinz, 5.3 oz, 130g) baked beans, grilled tomatoes, one banana.

Supper: One can slimmer's soup, any flavour, 4oz (100g) grilled lamb's liver, one grilled lamb's kidney, 4oz (100g) mushrooms poached in chicken stock, two rashers grilled streaky bacon, vegetables and/or salad from "free" list.

SUNDAY

Lunch: 3oz (75g) any lean roast meat with thin gravy OR casserole of 6oz (150g) any white fish cooked with low-calorie mushroom soup, onions, tomatoes, herbs, 2oz (50g) roast potato or 5oz (125g) jacket potato, vegetables from "free" list, 2oz (50g) peas, two slices pineapple, fresh or canned in juice with 1 tbs natural low-fat yogurt.

Supper: Any Findus Lean Cuisine or Weight Watchers from Heinz meal with salad from "free" list.

TREATS

Choose one every day:

One glass dry wine.

One half-pint (10fl oz) beer or lager

Two pub-measure "short" drinks

One crispy roll with salad from free list and 2oz (50g) prawns

One Mars Bar, Fun Size

Two fingers Kit Kat

Two digestive biscuits.

SWAP SPOT: You may swap any of your evening meals for a restaurant spread of melon, followed by grilled trout, sole or scampi with salad, then ice cream.

*RECIPES
BAKED FISH WITH BUTTER BEANS
Ingredients: 2 tbs (30ml) oil, four medium size mackerel or herrings, juice of 1/2 lemon, one 14oz (415g) can butter beans, drained, one large onion, peeled and chopped, 2 tbs parsley, chopped, salt and pepper to taste, 4 tbs (30ml) apple or pineapple juice.
Method: Heat the oven to 200°C/400°F, Gas Mark 6. Cut off heads and tails and gut fish. Wash thoroughly and dry. Open out on a board, press firmly and remove backbone and bones. Sprinkle inside with lemon juice, then close up fish. Slash one side of each fish with a sharp knife. Put beans, onion and herbs into a lightly greased oven proof dish. Arrange fish on top, pressing down slightly. Combine seasoning and juice with remaining oil and lemon juice. Spoon over the fish, cover with lid or foil and bake for 40 minutes.
SERVES: 4. Calories per portion: about 380.

FISH PLAKI
Ingredients: Four 6oz (150g) portions of any fresh white fish; one small green pepper, sliced; one medium onion, sliced; two cloves garlic, sliced

thinly; 1 tbs (15ml) olive oil; 14oz (400g) can tomatoes; one lemon, sliced; 2 tbs parsley, chopped; 1tsp dried thyme; salt; pepper.

Method: Gently soften onion and garlic in the olive oil. Drain off excess oil, then add the tomatoes, roughly chopped, the thyme, half the parsley and salt and pepper to taste. Bring gently to the boil and simmer for five minutes. Place the fish fillets in a baking dish, and pour over the tomato sauce, completely covering the fish. Scatter the slices of green pepper and lemon evenly over the mixture and place uncovered in the centre of a medium oven (180°C, 350°F Gas Mark 5) for 30 minutes or until cooked. Garnish with the remaining parsley. SERVES: 4. Calories per portion: 280.

FISH CREOLE

Ingredients: 4oz (100g) canned pineapple in natural juice, 2oz (50g) long-grain rice (dry weight), one tomato, skinned and chopped, one green and one red pepper, both chopped, 6oz (150g) any white fish; 1 tbs (15ml) lemon juice, seasoning, dash of Worcestershire or Tabasco sauce.

Method: Drain and chop pineapple and reserve juice. Make up to 1/4 pt (142ml) with water and cook the rice in this water for 7 minutes. Add

fish with lemon juice and water for 10-15 minutes, drain and flake. Stir into rice mixture. Season and add sauce to taste.
SERVES: 1. Calories per portion: about 400.

FOUR WEEK TAKE-AWAY DIET

Takeaways are a tasty treat enjoyed by everyone who likes an instant meal without spending time on its preparation. They are the busy person's answer to the problem of eating a reasonable meal without interrupting the work at hand for longer than it takes to eat it.

Takeaways are helpful, too, at times when you just want to slump in front of television after a long day and eat while you watch your favourite soap or sports programme. Their added plus is that you don't have to eat the same dish as your mate—great if one of you is a curry fan and the other prefers chow mein.

The downside is that most takeaways are high in calories. However, there is no reason why you shouldn't continue to enjoy those fast-food feasts while you diet.

Luckily, there is now a great deal of choice

available at fast food stops. And you don't HAVE to pick a greasy fry-up overloaded with chips!

By cutting calories at other meals you can balance your diet while still indulging your passion for pizzas, burgers, Chinese and Indian nosh-ups. This is less painful than it sounds!

This diet gives a set menu for breakfasts, a Light Meal and a Takeaway Meal each day. You can either eat your Light Meal at lunchtime, and your Takeway Meal at night—or the other way around. It's up to you!

The takeaway choices vary according to whether you intend to go for a pub meal, dine out at a pizza parlour, Indian or Chinese restaurant, grab a baked potato or have a meal at one of the big fast food chains like McDonald's or Burger King.

Try to ring the changes as much as possible and add plenty of "free" salads and vegetables to ensure that you get your fair share of vitamins and minerals. Your daily calorie intake is around 1250— which should produce a safe, steady weight-loss.

Follow the diet for two weeks, then repeat the whole plan for another fortnight.

WEEK ONE

Choose ONE takeaway meal every day from the list below:

One baked potato with coleslaw and prawns (Spud-U-Like), one apple.

A Kentucky Chicken Dinner For One with coleslaw and barbecued beans, one small banana.

One McDonalds Quarterpounder, one Diet Coke and one Shape yogurt.

Pub lunch of shepherd's pie, salad (no dressing), 1/2 pt beer or lager or two "short" drinks with low-calorie mixers or one glass dry wine with soda as a "spritzer".

One Wimpy Bacon and Egg in a bun, a few grapes.

One St Michael (or supermarket) turkey-and-ham or chicken-and-salad sandwich, one pear.

One ham and cheese croissant, one large banana, one apple.

One Indian meal of Chicken Tandoori, one poppadum, small serve plain boiled rice and salad (no dressing).

One Chinese meal of chicken or prawn chop suey, small serve plain boiled rice, lychees.

MONDAY

Breakfast: 1oz (25g) unsweetened cereal, milk from allowance, 1/4pt (142ml) orange juice.

Light Meal: Salad from "free" list with lemon juice and herb dressing; 3oz (75g) any cold meat, 4oz (100g) jacket potato with 1/4 oz (7g) low-fat spread, 1 tbs Branston pickle.

TUESDAY

Breakfast: One slice toast topped with 4oz (100g) baked beans.

Light Meal: Two fish fingers, 3oz (75g) oven chips, 3oz (75g) peas, vegetables and salad from "free" list.

WEDNESDAY

Breakfast: One size-3 egg, poached, on one slice toast with a little low-fat spread.

Light Meal: Any Findus Lean Cuisine or Weight Watchers from Heinz meal with vegetables from "free" list.

THURSDAY

Breakfast: One Weetabix, milk from allowance, one slice toast with 1 tsp (5ml) marmalade.

Light Meal: 10oz (250g) chicken leg, grilled or roast (no skin), salad from "free" list, one 7oz (175g) jacket potato.

FRIDAY

Breakfast: One rasher well-grilled streaky bacon,

Breakfast: One rasher well-grilled streaky bacon, grilled tomatoes, mushrooms poached in a little stock, two crispbreads with a little low-fat spread.

Light Meal: One packet Birds Eye Cod in Cheese, Butter or Mushroom Sauce, 3oz (75g) mashed potato (use skimmed milk for mashing), one orange.

SATURDAY

Breakfast: One slice toast topped with 4oz (100g) baked beans.

Light Meal: One two-egg omelette cooked in a non-stick pan with a little low-calorie spread and 1oz (25g) grated Edam cheese, salad from "free" list.

SUNDAY

Breakfast: 1oz (25g) bran cereal, milk from allowance, chopped apple on top.

Light Meal: 3oz (75g) any roast meat, 4oz (100g) jacket potato, thin gravy, vegetables from "free" list, a few grapes.

TREATS

Choose one every day:

1/2 pt beer or lager

One large glass dry wine

Two pub measure "short" drinks with low-calorie mixers

One diet yogurt, any flavour, and one banana

One Fun Size Mars bar

Two fingers of Kit Kat

WEEK TWO

Choose ONE takeaway meal every day from the list below:

Half medium pizza (e.g. Pizza Hut), salad from "free" list, one apple or orange.

One portion cod-in-batter from fish and chip shop, half portion chips, one orange.

Nine Chicken McNuggets, salad from "free" list, one apple.

One chicken or prawn salad sandwich, one packet low-fat crisps, one satsuma.

Pub lunch of steak and kidney pie, salad (no dressing) and one half-pint beer or lager OR one glass white wine "spritzer".

One cheeseburger and half portion chips.

One long French baguette filled with tuna and salad, one banana.

One Indian meal of chicken tikka or tandoori, small serve plain boiled rice, large mixed salad.

One supermarket Chinese meal OR chicken or prawn Chop Suey, plain boiled rice, lychees.

MONDAY

Breakfast: One Shape yogurt, any flavour, one banana.

Light Meal: One large slice melon, 4oz (100g) lean lamb chop, thin gravy, salad from "free" list, one apple.

TUESDAY

Breakfast: 1oz (25g) any unsweetened cereal, milk from allowance, one diet yogurt.

Light Meal: Any Findus Lean Cuisine or Weight Watchers from Heinz meal, with salad or vegetables from "free" list.

WEDNESDAY

Breakfast: One slice bread wrapped around one well-grilled chipolata sausage with 1 tsp (5ml) tomato sauce.

Light Meal: Half a grapefruit, Mexican Chilli Beef*, salad from "free" list.

THURSDAY

Breakfast: One apple and one banana chopped and served topped with 2 tbs natural yogurt.

Light Meal: Liver and Orange Casserole*, vegetables from "free" list.

FRIDAY

Breakfast: One size-3 poached egg on one slice toast.

Light Meal: Findus Prawn Curry with Rice or St. Michael Fisherman's Pie, vegetables and salad from "free" list.

SATURDAY

Breakfast: One slice toast topped with grilled tomatoes, 1/2 oz (15g) grated Edam cheese.

Light Meal: One 10oz (250g) chicken portion, grilled or roast, 7oz (175g) jacket potato, salad or vegetables from "free" list.

SUNDAY

Breakfast: Half a grapefruit, 1oz (25g) bran cereal, milk from allowance, a few grapes and 1 tbs natural yogurt.

Light Meal: 3oz (75g) any lean roast meat, 4oz (100g) jacket potato, thin gravy, vegetables from "free" list, a few grapes.

TREATS

Choose ONE every day:

One half-pint beer or lager

One large glass dry wine with soda water as a "spritzer"

Two pub-measure "short" drinks, with low-calorie mixers

Two digestive biscuits

Two After Eight mints

One tube Fruit Polos

One tin slimmer's soup, any flavour, with two crispbreads.

SWAP SPOT

You may swap any Light Meal for a carvery treat of chicken or turkey, vegetables from "free" list with ice cream or mousse to follow. Or, you may swap it for a steakhouse meal of melon, 6oz (150g) fillet steak or gammon and pineapple, with large mixed salad.

*RECIPES
MEXICAN CHILLI BEEF

Ingredients: one onion, chopped, 1 lb (450g) lean minced beef, 8 oz can tomatoes, 14oz (400g) can red kidney beans, drained; 1/2 tsp each cayenne pepper and chilli powder, 2 tbs (30ml) Worcestershire Sauce, salt and pepper.

Method: Place onion in a pan, add beef and fry for 5 minutes, stirring gently with a fork to keep separated. Stir in tomatoes, beans, cayenne, chilli powder, Worcestershire sauce. Cover and simmer for 30 minutes. Check seasoning and serve.

SERVES: 4   Calories per portion: about 340.

LIVER AND ORANGE CASSEROLE

Ingredients: 1lb (450g) lamb's or calf's liver, cut into slices and coated in seasoned flour; 1oz (25g) low-fat spread; one onion, chopped; one 15fl oz can ready-to-serve Mulligatawny soup; grated rind and juice of one orange. Garnish: One orange, watercress.

Method: Fry liver in the low-fat spread, place in an oven proof dish and keep hot. Gently fry onion for 5 minutes in the same pan. Add soup and grated rind and juice of one orange. Heat thoroughly and pour over the liver. Slice orange thinly and arrange on the liver. Garnish with watercress and serve.

THREE WEEKS TO SUPER-HEALTHY SLIMNESS

I f you want to look not only lean and lithe on the beach but bursting with glowing good health as well, try this delicious fruity eating plan.

In just three weeks leading up to the start of your holiday you could lose at least 8lb—and more if you step up regular exercise at the same time.

If you swim three days a week, say, then increase it to five days a week—or just double the length of your swim on your regular days. If you do virtually no exercise, go for a brisk 20 minute walk every second day. Or get off the bus or train one stop early on the way to or from work each day and walk the rest. Even running up and down stairs instead of taking the lift is a good way to increase fitness—though this is not suggested if you live at the top of a tower block! Better to do a supervised step class or use the step-machine at your local gym.

This diet makes the most of spring and summer

fruits and is packed with good things to help improve your skin, hair and vitality.

It also cheers you up by allowing a daily treat which can be a glass of your favourite tipple.

DAILY ALLOWANCES: One half-pint skimmed milk for your tea and coffee; unlimited water and mineral water; unlimited vegetables and salads from the "free" list on page 7.

CALORIES About 1350 daily. Men should add two extra slices wholemeal bread or one 8oz (200g) jacket potato, plus an extra half-pint of beer or lager.

WEEK ONE

MONDAY

Breakfast: One slice toast topped with two grilled tomatoes and 1/2 oz (12g) grated fat-reduced cheese, one quarter-pint (142ml) freshly-squeezed orange juice.

Lunch: One sandwich of two slices bread, salad from "free" list with 4oz (100g) cooked chicken (no skin), one apple.

Supper: Warm Egg and Bacon Salad* served with salad from "free" list, one 8oz (200g) jacket potato, one crusty roll with a little low-fat spread.

TUESDAY

Breakfast: One small, chopped banana, apple and pear topped with sprinkling of muesli and 2 tbs (30ml) natural yogurt, one slice toast with 1 tsp (15ml) honey.

Lunch: Pasta, Celery and Leek Soup*, two crispbreads with 1oz (25g) low-fat cheese spread, tomatoes, one large pear.

Supper: One large slice melon sprinkled with powdered ginger; one 8oz (200g) chicken joint, grilled or roast (no skin), vegetables and salad from "free" list, 3oz (75g) (dry weight) brown rice, one crusty roll, one carton natural yogurt with one chopped apple.

WEDNESDAY

Breakfast: One size-3 free-range egg, boiled or poached, one slice toast with a little low-fat spread, one pear.

Lunch: One crusty roll with filling of salad from "free" list, 3-1/2oz (100g) mashed tuna, lemon juice, one apple, one Leaf Lo Bar.

Supper: Spanish Pork* served with vegetables from "free" list, 4oz (100g) mashed potatoes (use skimmed milk for mashing), one carton diet yogurt.

THURSDAY

Breakfast: 1oz (25g) unsweetened muesli, milk from allowance, one chopped apple, one slice toast with Marmite.

Lunch: One sandwich of two slices bread, salad from allowance and 2oz (50g) lean ham, one diet fromage frais.

Supper: One 6oz (150g) serve any white fish, grilled with lemon juice and sliced tomatoes OR Curried Seafood Kebabs* served with 3oz (75g) cooked weight fluffy rice, salad from "free" list, one crusty roll, one baked appled stuffed with 1/2 oz (12g) raisins and 1 tsp (5ml) honey.

FRIDAY

Breakfast: Half a grapefruit, one grilled rasher back bacon, one grilled tomato, one slice of toast with a little low-fat spread.

Lunch: One wholemeal pitta bread stuffed with "free" salad, 2oz (50g) chopped, cooked chicken, one small sliced apple, lemon juice as dressing; one orange.

Supper: One can slimmers' soup, any flavour, two crispbreads, 4oz (100g) grilled liver with sage, thin gravy mixed with canned tomatoes, 3oz (75g) mashed potatoes (use skimmed milk from allowance for mashing), one huge portion "free" vegetables, one apple.

SATURDAY

Brunch: Pasta, Leek and Celery Soup*, one crusty roll, one apple, 10 grapes.

Supper: One 6oz (150g) serve lean, grilled steak with salad from "free" list, one 7oz (175g) jacket potato with a little low-fat spread. Nectarines in Peach Sauce*.

SUNDAY

Breakfast: 1oz (25g) muesli with milk from allowance, one slice toast with a little marmalade, one small glass freshly-squeezed orange juice.

Lunch: One 4oz (100g) serve any lean, roast meat, 3oz (75g) roast potatoes, 3oz (75g) carrots, thin gravy, vegetables from "free" list.

Supper: One slice toast topped with grilled tomatoes, 1oz (25g) fat-reduced cheese, two sliced kiwi fruit with one small banana.

TREATS

Choose ONE each day:

One glass dry wine OR two pub-measure "short" drinks with low-calorie mixers OR one half-pint beer or lager.

One crusty roll with salad filling from "free" list.

One mango, sliced and served with 1 tbs fromage frais.

One large banana.

One Fun Size Mars or Snickers bar.

One Leaf Lo bar.

WEEK TWO

MONDAY
Breakfast: One carton natural yogurt with chopped apple or pear, two crispbreads with a little low-fat spread and 2oz (50g) cottage cheese.
Lunch: One crispy roll with salad from "free" list and 1oz (25g) grated Cheddar cheese, one quarter-pint (142ml) glass tomato or apple juice, one apple or orange.
Supper: Slimmers' Chicken Korma*, 3oz (75g) (dry weight) pasta or rice, mixed salad from "free" list, a few grapes.
TUESDAY
Breakfast: One size-3 poached egg on one slice toast, one large glass freshly-squeezed orange juice.
Lunch: One sandwich of two slices bread with salad from "free" list and 2oz (50g) cooked chicken (no skin).
Supper: One 6oz (150g) serve any grilled white fish, one 7oz (175g) jacket potato, salad from "free" list, Coffee Yogurt Surprise*.
WEDNESDAY
Breakfast: One diet yogurt, any flavour, one slice toast topped with 1 tbs (15ml) peanut butter.
Lunch: One sandwich of two slices wholemeal

bread, salad from "free" list and 3-1/2 oz (100g) can tuna-in-brine, one apple.

Supper: One 5oz (125g) lean lamb chop, grilled, 1 tsp (5ml) mint sauce, 3oz (75g) mashed potato (use skimmed milk from allowance for mashing), 2oz (50g) peas, 2oz (50g) carrots, vegetables from "free" list, one orange.

THURSDAY

Breakfast: One grilled rasher back bacon, one slice toast, grilled tomatoes, one quarter-pint (142ml) glass of apple or grapefruit juice.

Lunch: One large slice melon, open sandwich of one slice bread, topped with "free" salad, 4oz (100g) cottage cheese and orange slices, one apple.

Supper: One 8oz (200g) chicken leg, grilled or roast (no skin) with tarragon, grilled tomato, 3oz (75g) (dry weight) brown rice or pasta, vegetables from "free" list, one diet yogurt, any flavour, one apple.

FRIDAY

Breakfast: 1oz (25g) any unsweetened cereal, skimmed milk from allowance, one chopped banana, two crispbreads with a little honey or marmalade.

Lunch: One sandwich of two slices bread with 2oz (50g) smoked salmon sprinkled with lemon juice, salad from "free" list, one large banana.

Supper: One large slice melon, 4oz (100g) (cooked weight) any pasta with sauce made from 2oz (50g) lean ham, cut in strips and mixed with canned tomatoes, garlic, herbs, lemon juice; salad from "free" list, Boozy Strawberries*.

SATURDAY

Brunch: Two slices wholemeal toast topped with grilled tomatoes, one egg, scrambled with a little low-fat spread and 1 tbs (15ml) sweetcorn, one chopped apple, pear and banana topped with 2 tbs natural yogurt or two squirts aerosol cream.

Supper: One 5oz (125g) serve lean rump steak, grilled, 3oz (75g) oven chips, vegetables and salad from "free" list, one apple.

SUNDAY

Breakfast: One Weetabix, milk from allowance, 4oz (100g) fresh or frozen berries (strawberries, blackberries, raspberries), one slice wholemeal toast with scraping of low-fat spread.

Lunch: 4oz (100g) any lean roast meat, 3oz (75g) roast potatoes, 3oz (75g) carrots, thin gravy, vegetables from "free" list.

Supper: One sandwich of two slices wholemeal bread, salad from "free" list and 1oz (25g) lean ham, one orange.

TREATS: As week one

WEEK THREE

MONDAY

Breakfast: One half small melon, deseeded, flesh chopped and mixed with one apple, 1/2 oz (15g) sultanas, 1oz (25g) muesli, piled back into shell and topped with one carton diet yogurt, any flavour.

Lunch: One sandwich of two slices wholemeal bread 2oz (50g) cooked chicken (skin removed), salad from "free" list, one pear.

Supper: Any Findus Lean Cuisine or Weight Watchers from Heinz ready meal with huge portion of "free" vegetables, one large pear.

TUESDAY

Breakfast: One size-3 free-range egg, boiled or poached, one slice wholemeal toast with a little low-fat spread, one large apple.

Lunch: One crusty wholemeal roll with filling of salad from "free" list, 2-1/2 oz (65g) mashed tuna-in-brine, lemon juice, one orange, one Leaf Lo bar.

Supper: Spanish Pork*, vegetables from "free" list, 3oz (75g) (dry weight) brown rice, salad from "free" list, one diet fromage frais.

WEDNESDAY

Breakfast: 4oz (100g) strawberries or raspberries on 1oz (25g) bran cereal, topped with 1 tbs (15ml) low-fat fromage frais.

Lunch: One sandwich of two slices wholemeal bread with "free" salad and 1oz (25g) grated fat-reduced Cheddar mixed with 1 tbs (15ml) low-calorie mayonnaise.

Supper: One large slice melon, Prawns With Spring Onion And Yogurt Dip*, one slice wholemeal bread, huge mixed salad from "free" list.

THURSDAY

Breakfast: Two Weetabix, milk from allowance, one small sliced banana, one quarter-pint (142ml) unsweetened grapefruit juice.

Lunch: 3-1/2 oz (100g) canned salmon, tuna or pilchard with huge mixed "free" salad, 1 tbs (15ml) low-calorie mayonnaise, one small crusty whole-meal roll.

Supper: Two pork chipolatas, well-grilled, thin gravy, grilled tomatoes, 3oz (75g) potatoes mashed with milk from allowance, one huge portion "free" vegetables, one apple.

FRIDAY

Breakfast: Two size-3 eggs scrambled with milk from allowance, served on one slice wholemeal toast with mushrooms poached in chicken stock or water, watercress, grilled tomatoes.

Lunch: One 8oz (200g) jacket potato with topping of 2 tbs (30ml) baked beans, huge mixed salad from "free" list, one diet yogurt, any flavour.

Supper: One 6oz (150g) serve any white fish, grilled, 2oz (50g) canned sweetcorn, two canned pineapple rings in natural juice, one huge portion "free" vegetables, 2oz (50g) vanilla ice cream.

SATURDAY

Brunch: Half grapefruit sprinkled with powdered ginger, two slices wholemeal toast topped with grilled tomatoes, 4oz (100g) cottage cheese, one rasher well-grilled streaky bacon, one quarter-pint (142ml) unsweetened orange juice.

Supper: Indian takeaway—Tandoori Chicken with salad, cucumber raita, one apple or orange OR a carvery meal of turkey or lean pork, "free" vegetables, fresh fruit salad.

SUNDAY

Breakfast: One small chopped banana, apple and pear topped with sprinkling of muesli and 2 tbs natural unsweetened yogurt.

Lunch: 4oz (100g) any lean roast meat, 3oz (75g) roast potatoes, 3oz (75g) carrots, thin gravy, vegetables from "free" list.

Supper: Warm Egg and Bacon Salad*, salad from "free" list, one quarter-pint (142ml) unsweetened orange juice.

TREATS: As week one.

RECIPES

PRAWNS WITH SPRING ONION AND YOGURT DIP

Ingredients: Eight large Mediterranean prawns; three spring onions; 4 tbs (60ml) Greek yogurt; seasoning; squeeze of lemon juice.

Method: Shell prawns but leave heads on. Remove the black vein that runs down the back of each prawn. Clean onions, chop the white parts finely and mix with the yogurt. Season to taste and stir in a small squeeze lemon juice. Arrange prawns on a large plate with dip in the centre.

Serves: 2. Calories per serving: 250.

PASTA, CELERY AND LEEK SOUP

Ingredients: Four celery sticks, chopped; two leeks, cleaned and sliced; one bunch watercress, washed and chopped; one round lettuce heart, shredded; four spring onions, chopped; 1 tbs (15ml) chopped fresh tarragon; one garlic clove, crushed; one pint (600ml) chicken stock; one half-pint (300ml) skimmed milk; salt and freshly ground black pepper; 2oz (50g) green ribbon pasta (fettucine) broken into short lengths, a little chopped parsley for garnish.

Method: Place celery, leeks, watercress, lettuce, spring onions, tarragon and garlic into a large pan. Add stock, skimmed milk and season to taste. Simmer for about 20 minutes until all the vegetables are tender. Blend in liquidizer until smooth. Return to pan, bring to the boil and add the pasta. Simmer about four minutes or until pasta is tender but not mushy. Serve piping hot garnished with chopped parsley.
Serves: 4. Calories per serving: 100.

WARM EGG AND BACON SALAD
Ingredients: Four size-1 eggs; 4oz (100g) lean bacon, diced; 2 tsp (10ml) each wine vinegar and mild mustard; 1 tsp (5ml) clear honey; pinch of salt; 8 fl oz (250ml) natural unsweetened yogurt; one round lettuce, washed and roughly chopped; 2 tsp grated Parmesan cheese; four slices wholemeal bread.
Method: Boil the eggs for six minutes. Fry the bacon gently in a non-stick pan until crispy. Leave to cool slightly. Add vinegar, mustard, honey, salt and yogurt to the bacon in the pan and stir well. Place the lettuce in a serving bowl, pour over the warm bacon dressing and toss. Rinse the eggs under cold water and remove shells. Quarter or, if preferred, chop into chunks. Place on salad and sprinkle over the

Parmesan. Serve with bread, toasted and cut into triangles.
Serves: 4. Calories per serving: 300.

CURRIED SEAFOOD KEBABS

Ingredients: 4 tbs (60ml) natural, unsweetened yogurt; 3 tbs lemon or lime juice; one clove garlic, crushed; 1 tsp curry powder; six drops Tabasco sauce; one thin slice fresh ginger, finely chopped; salt and freshly ground black pepper; 1lb (450g) firm white fish, cut into one-inch (2.5cm) cubes; 12 large peeled prawns; 12 shelled and rinsed mussels. Garnish: 1 tbs chopped fresh coriander; lemon or lime wedges.

Method: Mix the yogurt, lemon or lime juice, garlic, curry powder, Tabasco and chopped ginger. Season lightly. Stir the fish and shellfish into the mixture, cover and place in the refrigerator for three hours or overnight. Thread the fish and shellfish alternately onto four skewers and brush off any excess yogurt mixture. Place kebabs on a lightly greased baking sheet under a preheated grill. Grill for about six minutes, turning occasionally and brushing with marinade until fish is just tender. Serve on a platter sprinkled with coriander and lemon or lime wedges.
Serves: 4. Calories per serving: 170.

SPANISH PORK

Ingredients: 2lb (900g) pork fillet or tenderloin; 7oz (200g) onion, chopped; 1 tbs (15ml) olive oil; one clove garlic, crushed; one medium red pepper; one three-quarter pint (425ml) sieved tomatoes (passata, from most supermarkets); 8 fl oz (225ml) red wine; 4 fl oz (115ml) water; 8oz (225g) button mushrooms; 2oz (50g) pitted green olives; 6oz (150g) frozen petit pois; seasoning.

Method: Remove fat or sinew from pork and cut into thick slices. Cook the onion in the oil until soft and golden. De-seed the pepper and chop the flesh. Add garlic and pepper to the pan with the red wine, passata and water. Simmer, uncovered, for 15 minutes. Arrange the pork in a wide-base, shallow dish and pour the sauce over. Cover and cook at 350°F (180°C, gas mark 4) for 30 minutes. Add the mushrooms, olives and petit pois. Cover again and cook for a further 30 minutes or until meat is tender. Season to taste.

Serves: 6. Calories per serving: 295.

SLIMMER'S CHICKEN KORMA

Ingredients: 1 tsp ground cinnamon; six chicken drumsticks, skinned; three boned and skinned chicken breasts weighing about 5oz (125g) each, cut into cubes; one half-pint natural, unsweetened yogurt; 1 tbs (15ml) oil; two large onions, chopped; two fresh green chillis, seeded and chopped; 1 tsp cumin seed; one garlic clove, peeled and chopped; 1 tbs sweet paprika; 2 tbs (30ml) chicken stock; 1/2 tsp finely grated lemon rind; one red pepper, deseeded and chopped; 1 tbs cornflour; salt and freshly ground black pepper; freshly chopped coriander leaves for garnish.

Method: Rub the cinnamon into the chicken, pour over the yogurt and marinate for one hour in the refrigerator. Heat the oil in a casserole and lightly fry the onions, chillis, cumin and garlic. Stir in the paprika. Strain the chicken, reserving the yogurt marinade. Add the chicken to the casserole, stir well to coat with the onions, chillis and spices, then add the stock, lemon rind, red pepper and half of the yogurt marinade. Cover and simmer slowly, for about one hour. A few minutes before serving, combine the cornflour with the remaining yogurt, stir into the casserole, bring to the boil and simmer for about two minutes. Taste, season and serve garnished with coriander leaves.

Serves: 4. Calories per serving: 210.

NECTARINES IN PEACH SAUCE

Ingredients: One 15oz (425g) can peaches in juice; six nectarines; one strip of thinly pared orange rind;

3oz (75g) fresh or frozen blackcurrants, 2 tbs (30ml) apple juice; 2 tbs Hermesetas Sprinkle Sweet; 1 level tbs (15ml) Cassis; 2 tbs (30ml) Cointreau or Grand Marnier.

Method: Drain peaches and place the juice in a large pan with orange rind and nectarines in a single layer. Add enough water to just cover the fruit. Bring to the boil slowly. Cover and simmer gently for 10 minutes. Leave to cool in the juice. Meanwhile, cook the blackcurrants in the apple juice in a small covered pan until tender. Rub through a sieve and mix with 1 tbs Sprinkle Sweet and the Cassis. Puree the drained peaches with the orange liqueur and remaining Sprinkle Sweet. "Marble" the two fruit purees together in a serving dish. Peel the nectarines and serve in the sauces.

Serves: 6. Calories per serving: 150.

COFFEE YOGURT SURPRISE

Ingredients: One quarter-pint (142ml) strong black coffee mixed with artificial sweetener to taste; one half-pint (300ml) natural, unsweetened yogurt; one quarter-pint (142ml) skimmed milk; 3 tsp powdered gelatine; 3 tbs (45ml) water; four After Eight Mints and four squirts aerosol cream to garnish.

Method: Add the yogurt and milk to the coffee. Dissolve the gelatine in the water over a cup of hot water until clear. Add to the coffee mixture and mix thoroughly. Pour into four individual moulds and chill for about two hours until set. Unmould onto four flat serving dishes and garnish each one with a squirt of aerosol cream and an After Eight Mint. Serve immediately.

Serves: 4. Calories per serving: 120.

BOOZY STRAWBERRIES

Ingredients: 2-1/2 lb (1kg) ripe strawberries; two level tbs Hermesetas Sprinkle Sweet; 3 tbs (45ml) any liqueur such as Grand Marnier, Cointreau or Creme de Cassis; sprigs of mint for garnish.

Method: Puree 12oz (300g) of the fruit with the Sprinkle Sweet and liqueur. Place the remaining fruit in a glass serving dish and pour over the sauce. Garnish with mint.

Serves: 6. Calories per serving: 90.

TWO WEEK PACKED LUNCH DIET PLAN

S ticking to a diet during the working day can be a problem if the only food available is fattening pub grub, filling canteen nosh or sandwich-bar snacks designed to satisfy the heartiest appetite.

If you want to control the calories you consume while out at either work or play, the only thing for it is to take a packed lunch.

All these lunches can be packed up and taken wherever you go—which will leave you more time for holiday clothes shopping, and save cash for those two weeks in the sun!

You can even begin tanning in preparation for holiday beaches by taking your packed lunch to the nearest park and stretching out in the (if you're lucky) warm sunshine.

The Packed Lunch Plan gives a fast weight-loss— it provides about 1100 calories daily.

Follow the plan exactly for Weeks One and Two. If your holiday is more than two weeks away, you

can repeat the diet safely until you pack your bags
and take off.

EVERY DAY YOU CAN DRINK: One half-pint
(300ml) skimmed milk for your tea and coffee,
unlimited water, mineral water and diet soft drinks.

EVERY DAY YOU CAN EAT: As many "free"
vegetables as you like from the list on page 7.

WEEK ONE

BREAKFAST EVERY DAY (choose one from the
following list): One size 3 boiled egg, one slice
toast, half a grapefruit; 1/2 oz (15g) unsweetened
muesli mixed with one carton natural unsweetened
yogurt; two rashers well-grilled back bacon, two
grilled tomatoes, one crispbread; one quarter-pint
(142ml) unsweetened orange juice, 1oz (25g) unsweetened cereal or one Weetabix, a little skimmed
milk (extra to allowance).

MONDAY

Packed lunch: Sandwich of two slices bread with
lettuce, chopped hard boiled egg mixed with 1 tbs
(15ml) natural yogurt, finely chopped parsley, one
apple.

Supper: Four grilled fish fingers, 4oz (100g) mashed
potato (use skimmed milk for mashing), 2oz (50g)
each peas and carrots, plus vegetables and salad
from "free" list, one orange.

TUESDAY

Packed lunch: One crusty roll with salad from allowance and 3-1/2 oz (100g) tuna, 8oz (200g) carton Shape Reduced Calorie Coleslaw.

Supper: 10oz (250g) chicken portion, grilled or roast (no skin), 7oz (200g) jacket potato, salad from "free" list, one satsuma.

WEDNESDAY

Packed lunch: One mug Batchelor's Slim a Soup, any flavour; 4oz (100g) carton low-fat cottage cheese, one crusty roll with a little low-fat spread, salad from "free" list, one medium banana.

Supper: Four grilled beef chipolatas, small tin (5oz, 125g) baked beans, 3oz (75g) mashed potato (use skimmed milk for mashing), vegetables from "free" list, a few grapes.

THURSDAY

Packed lunch: One crusty roll with filling of salad from "free" list, 2oz (50g) prawns, 1 tbs (15ml) tomato chutney; 4oz (100g) carton St. Ivel Shape Potato Salad.

Supper: Any Findus Lean Cuisine or Weight Watchers meal, 5oz (125g) jacket potato, salad and/or vegetables from "free" list.

FRIDAY

Packed lunch: One 2oz (50g) piece French Bread with a

little low-fat spread, 1oz (25g) Cheddar cheese, two pickled onions, salad from "free" list.

Supper: 8oz (200g) any white fish, baked with tomatoes, onions and lemon juice, 3oz (75g) McCain Oven chips, salad or vegetables from "free" list, one pear.

SATURDAY

Lunch: Sandwich of two slices bread with 2oz (50g) cooked, diced chicken and chopped orange, plus salad from "free" list.

Supper: Spaghetti Bolognaise made from 2oz (50g) lean minced beef, small can tomatoes, sliced onion, garlic and herbs, served with 2oz (50g) (dry weight) pasta, 1 tbs (15ml) grated Parmesan cheese, salad from "free" list, two half-peaches (canned in juice, not syrup).

SUNDAY

Lunch: 3oz (75g) any lean roast meat, 2oz (50g) roast potato, 4oz (100g) carrots, thin gravy, vegetables from "free" list, one diet yogurt, any flavour.

Supper: One slice toast topped with one small can (e.g. Heinz, 7.6 oz) spaghetti in tomato sauce, one apple.

TREATS (Choose one each day):

One glass dry wine

One half-pint beer or lager

Two pub-measure "short" drinks
One Jacob's Club biscuit
Two fingers of Kit Kat.

WEEK TWO
BREAKFASTS EVERY DAY (choose one from
the following list):
One slice toast, topped with 1oz (25g) Edam cheese,
small sliced tomato
1oz (25g) any unsweetened cereal, a little skimmed
milk, one small chopped banana
Three crispbreads topped with Marmite and 3oz
(75g) curd cheese
1oz (25g) porridge oats made up with water, 1 tbs
(15ml) honey and skimmed milk from allowance,
one quarter-pint (142ml) unsweetened orange juice
Two Weetabix, 1 tsp sugar, a little skimmed milk,
one apple.
MONDAY
Packed lunch: One bread roll with 3oz (75g) any
roast meat, salad from "free" list, one pear.
Supper: One Ross Stir Fry Meal, any flavour, 2oz
(50g) (dry weight) rice, salad from "free" list.
TUESDAY
Packed lunch: One Scotch Egg, salad from "free"
list, one apple.

Supper: One 5oz (125g) lean lamb loin chop, thin gravy, vegetables from "free" list, 1oz (25g) vanilla ice cream.

WEDNESDAY

Packed lunch: One crusty roll with one chipolata sausage, well-grilled, 1 tbs (15ml) sweet pickle, salad from "free" list, one diet yogurt, a few grapes.

Supper: One pack Birds Eye Cod in Butter or Cheese sauce, 7oz (175g) jacket potato, 1oz (25g) peas, salad and vegetables from "free" list, a few grapes.

THURSDAY

Packed lunch: One 6oz (150g) jacket potato, middle scooped out and mixed with 1oz (25g) cubed Edam cheese, chopped tomato, celery; salad from "free" list.

Supper: Any Findus Lean Cuisine or Weight Watchers from Heinz meal, 3oz (75g) mashed potato (use skimmed milk for mashing), salad and vegetables from "free" list.

FRIDAY

Packed lunch: One sandwich of two slices bread, salad from "free" list, 3-1/2 oz (100g) can tuna (in brine) or pink salmon, lemon juice.

Supper: One Birds Eye Oven Crispy Cod Steak, 3oz (75g) McCain oven chips, 2oz (50g) peas, salad from "free" list, one apple.

SATURDAY

Lunch: One crusty roll with Marmite, 2oz (50g) cottage cheese, salad from "free" list, one diet yogurt.

Supper: One large slice melon, 6oz (150g) well-grilled rump steak, 5oz (125g) jacket potato, salad and vegetables from "free" list.

SUNDAY

Lunch: 3oz (75g) any lean roast meat, 2oz (50g) roast potatoes, 4oz (100g) carrots, thin gravy, vegetables from "free" list, one diet yogurt, any flavour.

Supper: Any supermarket own-brand Vegetable Lasagne, salad from "free" list, one orange.

TREATS

Choose one every day from this list:

One glass dry wine

One half-pint (10fl oz) beer or lager

Two pub-measure "short" drinks with low-calorie mixers

One Fun Size Mars bar

1oz (25g) Edam cheese with one crispbread

One diet yogurt and one pear

One crusty roll with a little low-fat spread and salad from "free" list.

SWAP SPOT

You may swap any of your evening meals for one of these:

One McDonald's Cheeseburger, one apple, one pear.

Carvery meal of chicken or turkey, vegetables from "free" list, mousse or ice cream.

Chinese meal of Chicken Chow Mein or Prawn Chop Suey, plain boiled rice, half portion beansprouts.

Italian meal of melon, veal with marsala, fresh fruit.

Pizza meal of half portion smallest-size pizza, salad from bar (no mayonnaise or other dressings).

TWO WEEK CHICKEN LICKIN' DIET

This is a great diet if you are off on a Mediterranean or Caribbean holiday. It includes lots of chicken—and turkey, which you probably won't be eating much on your hols! So, when you get to your destination you will taste the exotic fish and spicy meat dishes with extra enthusiasm.

White meat, such as chicken and turkey, is ideal slimmer's food because it is LOWER in calories than red meat. For instance, roast chicken (no skin) contains about 42 calories per ounce (25g), compared with 80 calories per ounce (25g) for roast sirloin of beef.

The Chicken Lickin' Diet also makes the most of the delicious ready-cooked white meat meals now available in the supermarkets. So you don't even have to consult a recipe or slice and weigh ingredients—leaving all the more time to practise such useful foreign phrases as "Make mine a tequila sunrise" or "What is the dish of the day, please?"

You are allowed 1100 Calories daily, which will give you a super weight-loss in time to look sleek in your swimsuit.But stick to it for two weeks ONLY.

WEEK ONE
BREAKFAST EVERY DAY
Choose ONE from the following list:

1oz (25g) any unsweetened cereal, milk from allowance, one quarter-pint (142ml) unsweetened orange juice

One size-3 poached egg, one slice toast with a little low-fat spread

One slice toast, 4oz (100g) baked beans.

MONDAY
Lunch: One crusty roll with salad from "free" list, one chopped hard-boiled egg mixed with 1 tbs (15ml) low calorie salad cream, one packet low-fat crisps.

Supper: St Michael Chicken Breasts in Spicy Indian Marinade, 7oz (175g) jacket potato, 1oz (25g) peas, vegetables from "free" list.

TUESDAY
Lunch: Sandwich of two slices bread, 1oz cheddar cheese, one tomato, one banana.

Supper: Chicken Curry*, 2oz (dry weight) (50g) rice, salad from "free" list.

WEDNESDAY

Lunch: One crusty roll with salad from "free" list, 2oz (50g) chicken or turkey, 1 tsp (5ml) sweet pickle, one diet yogurt, one small banana.

Supper: One Ross French Bread Pizza, any flavour, salad from "free" list, one apple.

THURSDAY

Lunch: One Golden Wonder Mushroom Pot Light, one apple.

Supper: One Dale Pak Turkey Steaklet, 3oz (75g) mashed potatoes (use skimmed milk for mashing), vegetables from "free" list, thin gravy, 1oz (25g) vanilla ice cream or Ross frozen mousse.

FRIDAY

Lunch: 3oz (75g) piece French bread, two chipolata sausages, 1 dsp (10ml) tomato ketchup, one pear.

Supper: 6oz (150g) white fish baked with lemon juice, sliced onion, tomatoes, herbs, 4oz (100g) mashed potato (use skimmed milk for mashing), 2oz (50g) peas, vegetables from "free" list, one small crusty roll.

SATURDAY

Lunch: Two slices toast with one small can (5oz, 100g) baked beans, one apple.

Supper: 10oz (250g) chicken portion with huge mixed salad from "free" list, one orange.

SUNDAY

Lunch: 3oz (75g) lean roast meat (no fat), 2oz (50g) roast potatoes, 2oz (50g) carrots, 1oz (25g) peas, thin gravy, vegetables from "free" list, one baked apple stuffed with 1/2 oz (15g) sultanas.

Supper: Findus Lean Cuisine Chicken and Prawn Cantonese, salad from "free" list, one diet yogurt.

TREATS

Choose one every day:

One glass dry wine

One half-pint beer or lager

Two pub-measure "short" drinks with low-calorie mixers

One Fun Size Mars or Snickers bar

One crusty roll with low-fat spread and salad from "free" list

One diet Ski yogurt and a small banana.

WEEK TWO:

BREAKFASTS EVERY DAY

Choose one from this list:

One Weetabix, milk from allowance, one slice toast with 1 tsp (5ml) marmalade

One large slice melon, one slice toast topped with grilled tomatoes

One size-3 poached egg, one rasher well-grilled streaky bacon, one crispbread.

1oz (25g) porridge oats made up with water, milk from allowance, one pear.

MONDAY

Lunch: One 7oz (175g) jacket potato or two small slices bread, filled with 2oz (50g) cooked cold chicken (no skin), 1 tbs sweet pickle, salad from "free" list, one tub Shape Coleslaw salad.

Supper: One Findus Crispy Chicken and Sweetcorn pancake; 3oz (75g) mashed potato (use skimmed milk for mashing), vegetables from "free" list, one crispy roll, 1oz (25g) vanilla icecream with 1 tsp jam mixed with a little hot water.

TUESDAY

Lunch: Sandwich of two slices bread, salad from allowance, 1oz (25g) cheddar cheese, one small banana.

Supper: One tin slimmer's soup, any flavour, one crispy roll, 3oz (75g) cold turkey or chicken with salad from "free" list, one 5oz (125g) jacket potato.

WEDNESDAY

Lunch: One Chicken and Mushroom Pot Noodle (Golden Wonder), one orange.

Supper: Two-egg omelette made in a non-stick pan with filling of 4oz (100g) mushrooms poached in stock, 3oz (75g) McCain oven chips, salad or vegetables from "free" list, one diet yogurt.

THURSDAY

Lunch: One crusty roll with salad from "free" list, 2oz (50g) cottage cheese, one carton diet coleslaw.

Supper: One Findus Lean Cuisine or Weight Watchers meal, any flavour, salad or vegetables from "free" list, one diet fromage frais.

FRIDAY

Lunch: 2oz (50g) chicken or turkey (no skin), 1 tsp mustard or sweet pickle, one carton diet coleslaw, one apple.

Supper: Chicken Curry*, salad from "free" list.

SATURDAY

Lunch: One tin slimmer's soup, any flavour, one slice toast topped with one small can (5oz, 125g) baked beans, one apple, one diet yogurt.

Supper: One large slice melon, two Matthews crispy crumb turkey steaks, grilled, 2oz (50g) mashed potato (use skimmed milk for mashing), salad from "free" list.

SUNDAY

Lunch: 3oz (75g) lean roast beef, lamb or pork (cut fat off, whichever you choose) or 3oz chicken (no skin), 2oz (50g) roast potatoes, 2oz (50g) carrots, 1oz (25g) peas, thin gravy, vegetables from "free" list, one baked apple stuffed with 1/2oz (15g) sultanas.

Supper: Two slices toast topped with one small tin (e.g. Heinz, 7.4oz) spaghetti, grilled tomatoes.

TREATS

Choose one each day:

One glass dry wine

One half-pint beer or lager

Two pub-measure "short" drinks with low-calorie mixers

Two fingers of Kit-Kat

Two crispbreads with low-fat spread, tomatoes and 1oz (25g) chopped chicken

Two After Eight Mints.

SWAP SPOT

You may swap any of your weekday suppers or Sunday lunches for one of these:

One portion Kentucky Fried Chicken, plus coleslaw

Carvery meal of chicken or turkey, "free" vegetables, ice-cream or mousse.

Pub meal of chicken-in-a-basket, jacket potato and salad.

Six Chicken McNuggets, salad and one banana.

Burger King hamburger in a bun, salad and one apple.

*RECIPES
CHICKEN CURRY.

Ingredients: 1/2 lb (225g) cooked, chopped chicken, 2oz (50g) onion, chopped; 1/2 clove garlic, crushed, 1 tbs curry powder, 1/2oz (15g) low-fat spread, 1/2oz (15g) flour; 1 tsp tomato puree, 3/4 pint (450ml) chicken stock, one small apple, chopped, salt.

Method: Cook onions, garlic and curry powder in the low-fat spread. Mix in the flour and cook. Blend in tomato puree and gradually add stock. Cook, stirring continuously until sauce is smooth. Add apple and chicken and cook for a further 30 minutes. Season and serve.

Serves: 2. Calories per portion: about 350.

TEN DAYS TO TAKE IT OFF!

You're booked on the tropical paradise holiday of a lifetime and you're counting the days till you're on the plane with a celebratory glass of bubbly in your hand.

Then, horror of horrors, you go shopping for a swimsuit. In the unflattering artificial light of a changing room you see only too clearly what has happened to your pretty good, standard-size 12 body in the past 12 months.

That normally taut tum and neat bum have been replaced by layers of lard. And the sexy little wiggle that has wowed them on the beaches since you were 16 is now just a great big horrible WOBBLE.

Are you ready for the big beach body exposure? Or do you just want to dive into a big hole in the sand? Or even cancel your tickets, go to Blackpool and pray for rain?

The sad thing about self-indulgence is it SHOWS. Even the most reliably normal-sized body will start to sag here and bulge there if over-fed and under-exercised for long stretches of time.

But you don't need me to go on about it—just tell you what you can do about this disaster in just 10 DAYS, right? Well, the first thing to say is: Don't panic! You can lose up to TEN WHOLE POUNDS of undesirable flab in just TEN days on our go-for-it diet.

Amazingly, you are even allowed goodies like booze, biscuits and chocs!

Too good to be true? Put it to the test by starting now—you've got nothing to lose but that blobby 10lb!

So, try on last year's bikini today, start the diet tomorrow—and try it on again in ten days' time. You'll be all ready to knock 'em dead with your slinky shape!

DIET RULES

1. Our plan allows about 1000 calories daily for women, 1300 for men. This is low—so do take a multi vitamin pill daily. And don't follow the diet for more than ten days.

2. You are allowed 1/2 oz (15g) low-fat spread (such as Gold or Outline) for bread and toast, and one half pint skimmed milk for your tea and coffee.

3. Each day, pick ONE breakfast, ONE Light Meal and ONE Main Meal plus TWO Treats.

4. Fellas, you are allowed an extra slice of bread or toast daily, and an extra Treat—lucky you!

5. You MUST drink eight glasses of water every day. This is to help you feel full, and to encourage your body to eliminate waste products (such as last night's curry!) Try to knock back a glass of mineral or tap water every hour throughout the working day.

6. You can also have unlimited veggies from the list on page 7.

7. No sugar allowed—sorry. Use sweeteners (such as Hermesetas) only.

8. Keep your mind busy—with work, holiday plans, fun. Go to the movies, read, re-vamp your CD collection. But DON'T overdo the exercise—this is no time to go jogging or join an advanced body-shaping class. (Swimming and sex are fine!).

9. Have a health or beauty treatment to make you feel great—a facial, hair-do, sunbed session, leg-wax or massage.

10. Slim with a partner. The one with the best shape gets a new swimsuit for the holiday!

BREAKFASTS
Choose ONE each day:
One low-calorie yogurt (Diet Ski, Shape), any

flavour, one slice toast with 1 tsp jam or honey, one large banana.

Two Weetabix, 1/4 pint (142ml) extra milk, a few grapes, 1/4 pt (142ml) unsweetened orange juice, one apple.

Two beef chipolatas, grilled, one poached size-3 egg, one grilled tomato, one crispbread.

1oz (25g) Special K cereal, 1 tbs each of chopped apple and pear, 3 fl oz (100ml) extra skimmed milk.

One boiled size-3 egg, one slice wholemeal toast, 1/4 pt (142ml) unsweetened grapefruit juice, one nectarine or peach.

8oz (200g) slice melon, seeds removed, flesh chopped and mixed with 1oz (25g) bran flakes, and topped with one carton natural yogurt

One slice wholemeal toast with Marmite, grilled tomatoes, one small carton cottage cheese, Worcestershire sauce, two satsumas.

LIGHT MEALS

Choose ONE each day:

One sandwich of two slices wholemeal bread, "free" salad, 2oz (50g) cottage cheese, one sliced tomato

One 8oz (200g) cold roasted chicken wing or leg, skin removed, a few grapes.

One small packet low-fat crisps, 1oz (25g) fat-reduced cheese, huge mixed salad using veggies from "free" list on page 7.

One can slimmer's soup, any flavour, 1oz (25g) cream cheese on two cream crackers, two pickled onions

4oz (100g) baked beans on one slice wholemeal toast, grilled tomatoes, mushrooms poached in water, watercress, huge mixed salad.

One tub Golden Wonder Pot Light, one apple or pear.

One sachet Batchelor's Slim a Soup, any flavour, one crusty roll with filling of "free" salad and cold chipolata sausage, 1 tsp (5ml) sweet pickle.

MAIN MEALS
Choose ONE each day:

One Findus Lean Cuisine or Weight Watchers from Heinz ready-meal, any variety, large portion green beans and cabbage, one satsuma.

6oz (150g) any grilled white fish, 3oz (75g) instant mashed potato, huge mixed salad with lemon juice and vinegar dressing

One beefburger, grilled, 4oz (100g) baked beans, 3oz (75g) instant mashed potato made up with milk from allowance.

Two-egg omelette (cook in a non-stick pan), 2oz (50g) oven chips

71

3oz (75g) roast chicken or turkey, one medium chunk roast potato, large portion green beans, sprouts and cabbage, thin gravy.

One Birds Eye Cod in Sauce, any variety, 4oz (100g) jacket potato, huge mixed salad with lemon juice dressing.

Six Chicken McNuggets, huge mixed salad with lemon juice dressing, one apple.

One can low-calorie soup, any variety, 4oz (100g) grilled bacon steak, 2oz (50g) sweetcorn, large portion "free" vegetables and salad.

One 8oz (200g) slice melon, 5oz (125g) grilled, lean chump chop or rump steak, large mixed salad.

TREATS

TWO each day for women, THREE for fellas:

One half pint beer, lager or stout
One glass dry wine
Two pub-measure "short" drinks
Three Rich Tea biscuits
One Fun Size Milky Way or Mars bar
One crusty roll with "free" salad
One Ferrero Rocher chocolate-covered hazelnut
Two After Eight Mints.

ONE WEEK CHIPS
ARE OKAY DIET!

Just a week to go before your holiday? You can shed 3lbs (1.5k) or more, in seven days by eating—weight for it—delicious chip butties! If you're the sort whose diets always fail because you can't give up that chips-with-everything habit, this is the diet for you.

This diet is also particularly useful if you are planning an action-packed break at a holiday camp or sports complex abroad. For skiers, windsurfers, mountain climbers, cyclists, hikers and all those whose idea of a great vacation means burning up energy at a furious rate, foods that boost stamina are of prime importance.

The Chips Are Okay Diet is NOT a seven-day feast of nothing but greasy chips piled between thick white bread slices slathered in butter. It simply uses two servings of chips each day as a supplement to the rest of the diet. And even though the chip butties are not the calorie-charged fried potato sandwiches famously from the north of England, they are tasty enough to satisfy the most enthusiastic chip butty fancier. In fact, many may find themselves preferring our diet version.

This week-long diet programme for those who favour strenuous exercise rather than lying round on beaches as a break from workaday life is high in complex carbohydrates. These help increase and sustain energy and are the main basis of foods like wholemeal bread, potatoes and pasta, all of which are filling as well as healthy. Athletes and sports people train on foods which are high in carbohydrates—and you'll not see many of them with thick waistlines or thunder thighs.

So take a tip from the streamlined and sporty and shape up for your high-energy hol by burning off some fat before you go. If you combine this diet with a daily bout of exercise—a brisk walk, jog, gym session or fitness workout that is part of your normal exercise routine—you'll not only lose that extra weight but be extra fit for your well-earned break.

Sorry, there is no alcohol for the girls, and just one half-pint daily for the fellas. Drink loads of water instead—you'll enjoy those holiday tipples that much more when the time comes!

Here's how The Chip Butty Diet works:

You're allowed TWO portions of chips EVERY DAY. And YOU can choose how and when you'd like them. You can even have a chip butty for an afternoon snack if that's what takes your fancy! Or you can include a portion of chips with your lunch or supper.

What matters is that you use oven chips rather than fries, and that you stick to the right-sized portions. But as long as you keep to the rules, you can indulge your chip habit daily and still lose weight.

EACH DAY you are allowed half a pint of skimmed milk, plus UNLIMITED water, mineral water, diet soft drinks, black coffee and lemon tea, green vegetables and salads such as lettuce, cucumber, cabbage, courgettes, cauliflower and peppers. Check with the free list on page 7 for the full range of choices.

Remember to use only lemon juice on salad—no oil! And leave out the butter when you tuck into your vegetables—toss them in lemon juice instead, and add some chopped parsley or coriander for a delicious buzz of extra flavour.

Now pick ONE breakfast, ONE lunch and ONE supper each day from the list that follows. You'll find it easier to stick to the diet if you go for different choices each day, so that no two days are ever the same. And varying your choices will mean that you are sure of the right balance of vitamins and minerals.

Fellas can add half a pint of beer or lager and two extra slices of bread and low-fat spread to their daily menu.

BREAKFASTS:

A medium-sized egg, poached or boiled, and a slice of wholemeal toast.

1oz (25g) muesli mixed with a sliced small banana, or grated apple, and milk from allowance.

1oz (25g) low-fat cottage cheese spread on a slice of wholemeal toast, topped with sliced tomato, and grilled.

1 grilled chipolata sausage, grilled tomatoes, two crispbreads thinly spread with low-fat spread.

1 small glass of fruit juice, a slice of wholemeal toast thinly spread with honey.

Half a grapefruit, 1oz (25g) any unsweetened cereal, milk from allowance.

LUNCHES:

Sandwich made from two slices of wholemeal bread plus any of the following fillings:

2oz (50g) cottage cheese with salad

1oz (25g) smoked salmon sprinkled with pepper and lemon juice

1oz (25g) lean ham with salad

1 rasher grilled back bacon, lettuce and tomato

OR one cup of slimmer's soup, one chip butty*

OR try any of the following with a large mixed salad and ONE of your two daily allowances of chips—remember, 2oz (50g) oven chips only, NOT FRIED:

6oz (150g) grilled or poached chicken, skin removed.

Two well-grilled chippolata sausages,

Three grilled fish fingers

SUPPERS

Greek Meatballs*, Home-made Tomato Sauce*, mixed salad, a few grapes

Jamaican Chicken*, mixed salad, apple chopped in low-fat yogurt

Normandy Pork Chops*, 4oz (100g) potato baked in its jacket, with low-fat yogurt and chives, baked apple with creme fraiche

5oz (125g) grilled rump steak, ONE of your two

daily allowances of oven chips, huge mixed salad, a pear
3oz (75g) any cooked, lean meat, thin gravy, large portion of green vegetables

SNACK (any time, but ONCE A DAY ONLY!)
Chip butty, but ONLY if you haven't used up your chip allowance elsewhere!

DAILY CALORIES
Girls, about 1300. Fellas, about 1600.

*RECIPES

CHIP BUTTY
Make a sandwich with two small slices wholemeal bread, 2oz (50g) oven chips, vinegar and a little salt and pepper to taste.

GREEK MEATBALLS
Ingredients: 1 lb (450g) lean minced beef or lamb; 1 medium onion, finely chopped; 2 slices bread crumbled into breadcrumbs; 1 tsp dried thyme; 1 tsp dried oregano; one egg, beaten; salt, pepper; 2 tbs chopped parsley.
Method: Combine the mince, breadcrumbs, finely chopped onion, thyme, oregano, salt, pepper and half the parsley. Mix well until all the ingredients

are evenly distributed. Add the beaten egg, and mix some more. Divide the meat mixture into eight equal portions, and roll each portion into a ball. Place the meatballs under a hot grill for 10-15 minutes, turning once (or, better still, grill the meatballs on a barbecue). Garnish with the remaining parsley.

Serves 4. Calories per serving: 310

HOME-MADE TOMATO SAUCE

Ingredients: 1 tsp (5ml) olive or other vegetable oil; two cloves garlic, crushed; 14oz tin chopped tomatoes; 1 tbs wine vinegar; salt, pepper; 1/2 tsp chilli powder (optional).

Method: Heat the oil gently in a saucepan, add the garlic and stir for two minutes. Then add the chopped tomatoes, salt, pepper and the optional chilli powder if you like your sauces hot! Bring to the boil, and allow the liquid to boil away until you are left with a bit over half the quantity you started with. Now add the wine vinegar, and simmer for another five minutes. As well a being a brilliant accompaniment to Greek meatballs, this sauce is delicious with grilled sausages, grilled chicken, even grilled fish. It contains very few calories, so use it to give sparkle to otherwise plain diet dishes.

Serves 4. Calories per serving: 20.

JAMAICAN CHICKEN

Ingredients: Four 6oz (150g) chicken portions, with skin removed; 1 tsp curry powder; 1 tsp ground coriander; 1 inch (2.5cm) fresh ginger root, finely chopped; 8oz (200g) can pineapple chunks in unsweetened juice; 1 green pepper, chopped finely; salt, pepper.

Method: Mix the coriander and curry, and rub it over the chicken pieces. Place the chicken pieces in a shallow dish and pour over the strained juice from the pineapple tin, and add the chopped ginger. Marinate in a refrigerator for at least two hours. Grill the chicken pieces for 20-25 minutes, turning them several times and basting them with the marinade to stop them becoming dry. Meanwhile, use a blender to liquidise a mixture of the pineapple bits, any leftover marinade and the chopped pepper. Pour the blend into a saucepan and heat through, adding salt and pepper to taste. Place the grilled chicken portions on plates, pour the hot sauce over them. Serves 4. Calories per serving: 225.

NORMANDY PORK CHOPS

Ingredients: 4 medium pork chops, with fat trimmed off; medium onion, finely chopped; 2 cloves garlic, crushed; 2 tbs parsley, finely chopped; 1/4 pint (142ml) dry cider.

Method: combine the finely chopped onion, crushed

garlic and half the parsley. Spread half the mixture on one side of the chops and grill this side for 12-15 minutes. Turn over, spread the rest of the mixture on the chops, and grill for a further 12-15 minutes. Transfer the chops to a frying pan. Drain any excess fat from the grill pan, add the 1/4 pint (142ml) dry cider and stir well with a wooden spoon until the pan juices have blended with the cider. Pour this mixture over the chops in the frying pan, and boil for 3-4 minutes until liquid is reduced by half. Serve chops with liquor, and garnish with remaining parsley.
Serves 4. Calories per serving: 215

CHINESE PORK
Ingredients: 12oz (300g) lean pork, cut into strips; 2 tbs (30ml) groundnut oil; small Chinese cabbage, shredded; 1 tbs chopped hazelnuts; 4oz (100g) bean shoots; 2 tbs (30ml) soy sauce; 1 tsp curry powder; 1/4 tsp chilli powder; 1/4 tsp brown sugar; salt, pepper.
Method: Heat oil in frying pan or wok, add the pork, and stir-fry until thoroughly browned. Season with salt and pepper. Add the cabbage, hazelnuts and a wineglass of water, and simmer for five minutes, stirring continuously. Add the bean shoots, soy sauce, curry powder, chilli powder and sugar, stir and simmer for a further 10 minutes.
Serves 4. Calories per serving: 210

ONE WEEK HIGH FIBRE SUPER ENERGY DIET

You'll feel full of beans and look like a star on holiday if you boost your energy-rating and whittle down your waistline on our great seven-day streamliner diet.

What's more, you'll hardly know you're dieting as you tuck into loads of deliciously filling baked beans, piles of satisfying spuds and mountains of fresh-tasting fruits and vegetables.

Hunger pangs will be kept at bay by the high fibre content of the foods you will be savouring at every mealtime. So by the end of the week you are likely to be amazed by a weight loss of up to 4lbs—which you will feel you've lost without even trying!

On top of that, you'll feel full of bounce and raring to take off on that action-packed holiday. Whether you're scuba-diving, pony trekking, windsurfing or skiing you'll have no trouble keeping up the pace.

EVERY DAY: Choose one breakfast, then follow the day's lunch and supper menus exactly. Pile on the "free" vegetables from the list on page 7. You can also add two treats each day from the list below. And allow one half-pint of skimmed milk each day for your tea and coffee.

BREAKFASTS

Choose ONE each day from the following list:

One quarter-pint (142ml) unsweetened fruit juice, 1oz (25g) unsweetened cereal served with one quarter-pint skimmed milk EXTRA to allowance.

One 5oz (125g) slice of melon, one slice wholemeal toast, 2 tsp (10ml) low-fat spread, 2 tsp (10ml) marmalade.

Half a medium grapefruit, 1oz (25g) hard cheese on a slice of wholemeal toast.

One quarter-pint (142ml) unsweetened fruit juice, one slice of wholemeal toast, 2 tsp (10ml) low-fat spread, 3oz (75g) baked beans.

One quarter-pint (142ml) unsweetened fruit juice, one size-3 egg, boiled or poached, one slice of wholemeal toast with thin scraping of low-fat spread.

One small orange, two sardines on one slice of wholemeal toast with thin scraping of low-fat spread.

One 1oz (25g) serve unsweetened bran cereal, milk from allowance, one small banana.

DAY ONE

Lunch: One 3oz (75g) serve baked beans, one slice wholemeal toast, 2 tsp low-fat spread, mixed salad from "free" list, small carton low-fat fruit yogurt, any flavour.

Supper: One 4oz (100g) salmon steak or mackerel fillet, grilled, OR Salmon Surprise*; 6oz (150g) boiled new potatoes tossed in 1 tsp (5ml) lemon juice and 1 tsp finely chopped mint and parsley, huge portion "free" vegetables; one apple.

DAY TWO

Lunch: 3oz (75g) tuna mashed with 1 tsp (5ml) low-calorie seafood sauce, two crispbreads, 1 tsp (5ml) low-fat spread, celery and watercress, one medium apple.

Supper: Two low-fat, well-grilled sausages OR Sausages in Cider*; 6oz (150g) mashed potato with milk from allowance, 4oz (100g) peas, huge portion "free" vegetables and salad, one orange.

DAY THREE

Lunch: One 8oz (200g) jacket potato, 2oz (50g) cottage cheese with chives, "free" salad, 4 tsp (20ml) low-calorie mayonnaise, one orange.

Supper: One 3oz (75g) portion lean grilled pork tenderloin or lamb chop OR Spicy Lamb Kebab*; 6oz (150g) potato mashed with milk from allowance, huge portion "free" vegetables, one small bunch grapes.

DAY FOUR

Lunch: One sandwich of two slices wholemeal bread, 1oz (25g) cooked chicken (no skin), "free" salad, one packet low-fat crisps, one orange.

Supper: Four fish fingers, grilled, OR Herby Fishcakes*; 4oz (100g) baked beans, 6oz (150g) mashed potato with milk from allowance, loads of "free" salad and vegetables, one pear.

DAY FIVE

Lunch: One wholemeal pitta bread stuffed with "free" salad and 2oz (50g) mashed tuna or sardines with plenty of lemon juice, one diet yogurt, any flavour.

Supper: Broccoli and Cheese Souffle*, fresh fruit salad made from one chopped banana, one sliced kiwi fruit, a few grapes and raspberries, topped with one carton natural unsweetened yogurt.

DAY SIX

Lunch: One mug Batchelors Slim-a-Soup, any flavour, one wholemeal roll with fillng of "free" salad and 1-1/2oz (40g) low-fat soft cheese, one large pear.

Supper: One 5oz (125g) portion lean rump steak, well-grilled, 3oz (75g) oven chips, huge portion of "free" vegetables, Banana Delight*.

DAY SEVEN

Lunch: One slice melon, 3oz (75g) any lean, roast meat (hot or cold), 8oz (200g) jacket potato, loads of "free" vegetables, 2oz (50g) sweetcorn, small bunch grapes.

Supper: Two slices wholemeal toast topped with 6oz (150g) baked beans, watercress, grilled tomatoes, one orange.

TREATS

Choose TWO each day:

One glass dry wine OR one half-pint beer or lager
One small packet low-fat crisps
One large banana

*RECIPES

SALMON SURPRISE

Ingredients: Four 4oz (100g) salmon steaks; 1lb (450g) fresh or frozen spinach; juice of one half lemon, four lemon slices; fresh tarragon; salt, pepper. Garnish: Diced fresh tomato tossed in lemon juice, black pepper, pinch of cayenne pepper or few drops Tabasco.

Method: Heat oven to 180°C, 350°F, gas mark 4. Cook spinach in a saucepan with very little water and a little salt until just tender enough to chop or puree. Divide spinach into four and spread each portion on piece of foil large enough to loosely wrap around the fish. Place fish on top of spinach, sprinkle with salt, pepper and chopped tarragon leaves plus a slice of lemon. Wrap and place parcels on baking tray and cook in pre-heated oven for 20 minutes. Remove from foil and serve with fresh tomato garnish.

Serves: 4. Calories per serving: 290.

SAUSAGES IN CIDER

Ingredients: 1lb (450g) pork chipolata sausages; two shallots, finely chopped; two Granny Smith apples, peeled, cored and sliced; 1 tsp dried sage or 1 dsp chopped fresh sage leaves; one clove garlic, finely chopped; one quarter-pint (142ml) dry cider; salt and pepper.

Method: Pre-heat oven to 180°C, 350°F, gas mark 4. Prick sausages and lightly grill them. Place on kitchen towel to drain them of excess grease. Put sausages in casserole dish, cover with shallots, apples, sage, garlic, pepper and salt. Pour cider over, cover with lid and cook in oven about 35 minutes, till apples are soft and form a thick sauce with the cider. Cook for last five minutes or so with lid off.

Serves: 4. Calories per serving: 290.

SPICY LAMB KEBABS

Ingredients: 1lb (450g) lean lamb, diced in one-inch (2.5cm) cubes; one large courgette, thickly sliced; 8oz (225g) button mushrooms; one small onion, grated; one crushed clove garlic; 1/2 tsp each ground ginger and coriander; 1 tsp cumin; one-quarter tsp cinnamon; juice of one lemon; one small carton unsweetened natural yogurt; salt and pepper.

Method: Mix all ingredients except lamb, courgette and mushrooms in a bowl to make marinade. Add diced lamb and stir it round till well-covered. Cover and put in fridge for at least two hours (overnight is fine). When wanted, thread on four skewers along with courgette chunks and washed and dried mushrooms. Drizzle any marinade left in bowl over kebabs and cook under hot grill till meat is browned and cooked according to taste.

Serves: 4. Calories per serving: 285.

HERBY FISHCAKES

Ingredients: 8oz (225g) any white fish, minus skin and bones; 8oz (225g) mackerel, skin and bones removed; 3oz (75g) grated onion; 3oz (75g) grated carrot; 1 dsp finely chopped dill; 1oz white breadcrumbs; one beaten egg; juice of half a lemon, plus grated lemon rind; salt and freshly ground black pepper.

Method: Place all ingredients in bowl and mash together thoroughly till you can shape the mixture into eight half-inch thick rounds. Place them on a foil-lined grill-pan and cook under griller for about seven minutes each side.

Serves: Four. Calories per serving: 175.

BROCCOLI AND CHEESE SOUFFLE

Ingredients: 1lb (450g) broccoli; salt; 2 tbs low-fat spread; 2 tbs plain flour; one quarter-pint (142ml) skimmed milk; 3 tbs (45ml) dry white wine; freshly ground black pepper; four eggs, separated; three anchovy fillets, chopped (optional); 3 tbs (45ml) grated Parmesan cheese; 2 tbs wholemeal breadcrumbs.

Method: Pre-heat oven to 375°F, 190°C, gas mark 5. Cook the broccoli in boiling salted water until tender. Drain thoroughly and liquidize. Heat the low-fat spread in a pan, stir in the flour and cook for one minute. Gradually stir in the milk and wine. Bring to the boil, stirring until the sauce has thickened. Add the broccoli puree, season to taste, then add egg yolks, 2 tbs (30ml) Parmesan and anchovy fillets if used. Grease a 2-1/2 pint (1.5 litre) souffle dish with a little low-fat spread and sprinkle in the breadcrumbs. Whisk the egg whites until stiff, fold lightly but thoroughly into the broccoli mixture. Transfer to prepared souffle dish and sprinkle with remaining cheese. Bake in pre-heated oven for 25 to 30 minutes until risen and golden. Serve immediately with a huge salad from "free" list.

Serves: 4. Calories per serving: 350.

BANANA DELIGHT

Ingredients: 3 tbs Hermesetas Sprinkle Sweet; 12oz (350g) Greek yogurt; 4oz (100g) chocolate digestive biscuits; six medium bananas; 1 tbs (15ml) lemon juice; one kiwi fruit.

Method: Stir the Sprinkle Sweet into the Greek yogurt. Crush the biscuits. Peel and slice bananas and mix with the lemon juice. Layer yogurt, biscuit crumbs and bananas in six glasses. Decorate with sliced kiwi fruit.

Serves: 6. Calories per serving: 150.

THREE-DAY EMERGENCY DIET!

A spur of the moment decision to fly away for a long weekend—or a week or more—can catch you at one of those moments when you just wish you hadn't kept putting off that decision to lose a pound or two.

Whenever we put on a few unwanted pounds, most of us intend to get rid of them before things get out of hand. But so often we don't get round to it. That's when a last-minute trip or surprise party invitation has us gnashing our teeth and wondering if a few days' starvation will do the trick?

No need to get that drastic. You can smooth out those small-but-hated bulges by sticking to my magic Veggie Plan which can work wonders in JUST THREE DAYS. You'll save both cash and calories with this green-and-mean regime!

Just seventy-two hours before take-off is all you need to get you into good shape before you go. You could lose up to 4lbs—and THAT will mean the difference between showing off in your favourite slinky good-time wear or hiding your shape under something loose.

But one word of warning: don't blow your three-day emergency effort before you even reach your destination. Stuffing yourself with airline food and booze would be a tragic waste, wouldn't it? Instead, pace yourself carefully during your break.

If you are going to the sun, take advantage of the delicious local fruits and vegetables. If it's a city break, choose sensible items from restaurant menus using the calorie guide on page 95. And try to keep alcohol to a minimum! One glass of bubbly is all you need to put you in holiday mood each day!

Ready, steady, countdown...

EVERY DAY: Drink plenty of water and mineral water. You can also have one glass dry wine or one half pint (10fl oz) beer or lager or two pub-measure "short" drinks with low calorie mixers.

Now choose ONE Fruity Breakfast, ONE Leafy Lunch and ONE Nutty Supper from the following lists:

FRUITY BREAKFASTS
One apple, one banana, one slice of wholemeal toast with a little honey.

One medium glass orange juice, one half- slice toast topped with tomatoes and sprinkling of dried nuts. One shredded wheat with a little soya milk, sliced peach and apple.

LEAFY LUNCHES
One sandwich of two slices bread, lettuce, tomato, cucumber and ONE of the following:
 3 tbs (45ml) baked beans
One small carton St. Ivel Shape Coleslaw
One heaped tsp peanut butter
1oz (25g) vegetable paté
OR
A large mixed salad with lemon juice dressing plus one 10oz (250g) jacket potato topped with 1/2oz (15g) low-fat spread and one apple or orange.

NUTTY SUPPERS
One Dalepak Vegetable Burger, one large portion green vegetables sprinkled with 1 heaped tsp (10ml) mixed nuts, 5oz (125g) jacket potato, grilled tomato, one apple
One 2oz (50g) slice Granose Nut Loaf, one small tin spaghetti in tomato sauce, large mixed salad, one scoop vanilla ice cream with 4oz (100g) frozen raspberries and a little grated chocolate

Two slices toast topped with small can baked beans, grilled tomatoes, 5oz glass of soya milk whisked up with one medium banana and 1 tbs wheatgerm.

One can Heinz Farmhouse Chicken and Vegetable Whole soup sprinkled with 1 heaped tsp (10ml) nuts, one wholemeal roll, 10oz (250g) jacket potato with a little low-fat spread, large mixed salad, one apple or pear.

Fellas: Each day you can add an extra half pint bitter or lager, two extra slices wholemeal bread with low-fat spread, and a bigger portion of nuts!

CALORIES: About 1000 daily for women, 1500 for men.

CALORIE GUIDE TO HOLIDAY FOOD

In great shape for your holiday? By all means tuck in to all the local delicacies—but try not to blow all your hard work by eating all the wrong things when you get there.

Instead, use the calorie guide below to check out the fattening power of all those delicious foreign dishes. Make sure you eat (and drink!) sensibly. Have breakfast every day, enjoy a salad or fishy lunch and have a long, lingering evening meal.

Avoid fatty, greasy and sweet foods, eat lots of fruit and choose leaner cuts of meat. Keep booze down to a reasonable level, and always order bottled water with your meal, so you can make every other tipple a low-calorie one!

A sensible calorie allowance would be:

Breakfast—350 Calories
Lunch—450 Calories
Evening Meal—600 Calories
Drinks and Snacks—600 Calories
That's a total of 2000 Calories

If you take plenty of exercise, you should keep your weight steady. Who knows—you could even lose a pound or two!

FRANCE:

Starters:	Calories
Coquilles St. Jacques (scallops with cheese and potato sauce)	360
French Onion Soup	275
Fish Soup	220
(with croutons, mayonnaise, Gruyère cheese)	500
Mushrooms à la Greque	120
Moules Marinières	180

Main Courses:	
Boeuf Bourguignonne	520
Coq au Vin	630
Duck in Orange Sauce	700
Grilled Sole	320
Grilled Trout	280
Steak au Poivre	480

Desserts:	
Crêpes Suzette	420
Chocolate Mousse	260

Pineapple with Kirsch	95
Profiteroles	650

Good meal choice: Mushrooms à la Greque, Grilled Trout, Pineapple with Kirsch.

GREECE

Starters

Dolmades (stuffed vine leaves)	175
Fried Kalamari	550
Houmous with Pitta Bread	480
Marinaded Kalamari	200
Taramasalata with Pitta Bread	450
Tzatziki with Pitta Bread	290

Main Courses

Lamb Kebabs	350
Meatballs	575
Moussaka	675

Extras:

Olives (one)	3
Greek salad with Fetta Cheese	185
Baklava (layered pastry with walnuts and honey)	380
Halva	250

Good meal choice: Dolmades, Greek Salad, Lamb Kebabs.

ITALY

Starters:

Cannelloni	320
Lasagne	450
Seafood salad	230
Melon with Parma Ham	160
Minestrone Soup	130
Spaghetti Carbonara	520

Main Courses:

Cannelloni	500
Calves Liver with Sage	375
Lasagne	650
Seafood salad	370
Ravioli	520
Spaghetti Bolognese	750
Spaghetti Carbonara	1040
Squid in Red Wine with Onions and Tomato Sauce	300

Pizzas:

Thin crust, medium size:

Ham and Mushroom	750

| Seafood | 650 |
| Cheese and tomato | 700 |

Desserts:

| Cassata Ice cream | 150 |
| Figs | 60 |

Good Meal choice: Melon with Parma Ham, Seafood Salad, Figs

SPAIN AND PORTUGAL

Starters:

Prawns in Garlic	212
Gazpacho	100
Chorizo Sausage	180
Melon	60
Caldo Verde (Cabbage and Potato Soup)	125
Grilled Sardines	120

Main Courses:

Paella Valenciana	780
Tortilla (Spanish omelette)	450
Bacalhau (dried cod)	
with potatos and olives	630
Zarzuela de Mariscos (shellfish stew)	450

Desserts:

Flan de Arroz al Limon (rice and lemon caramel custard)	230
Lemon sorbet	100

Good meal choice: Melon, Zarzuela de Mariscos, Lemon Sorbet.

USA

Burgers and accompaniments:

Big Mac	485
Burger King Whopper	780
Portion of Fries	536
Hash Browns	250
Milk Shake, any flavour	400
Danish Pastry	450
Doughnut	295

Steakhouses:
Starters:

Potato skins with cheese	360
Deep Fried Mushrooms	315
Fruit Juice	55
Chicken Soup	60

Main Courses:

12oz (340g) Rump Steak	940
T-Bone Steak	1020
Mixed Grill	900
Rack of Lamb	790
Spare Ribs in Barbecue Sauce	1010
Barbecued Chicken	400

Side Orders and Extras:

French Fries	350
Jacket Potato	250
Garlic Bread	335
Blue Cheese Dressing	250

Desserts:

Chocolate Fudge Dessert	640
Brownies with Cream	620
Blueberry Pie with Cream	550

Good Meal Choice: Chicken Soup, Barbecued Chicken, Jacket Potato, Salad, no dressing!

UNITED KINGDOM

Starters:

Prawn cocktail	350
Tomato soup	150
Fruit juice	55

Main course:

Rump steak	300
Roast pork, apple sauce and gravy	350
Fried plaice with tartare sauce	575
Roast chicken	275
Jacket potato	160
French fries	320
Peas	50

Dessert:

Apple pie and custard	400
Ice cream	200
Fresh fruit salad	100

Snacks:

Ice cream cornet	145
Candyfloss	60
Jellied eels	132

Good Meal Choice: Fruit Juice, Roast Chicken with Jacket Potato, Fresh Fruit Salad.

THE CALORIE TRAP CAN UNDO YOUR DIET

Y ou're home from your hols and looking good—slim, fit, a healthy tan, shiny eyes, ready to face the world with new sparkle and energy.

Most of all, you want to keep that leanline body you were so proud of by the pool, on the ski slopes, on the tennis court or sauntering along the boulevards of your favourite holiday city. We all come home full of the best intentions. But how long does it take before those old, sloppy habits creep back into our lives? We resolve to eat a sensible, nutritious breakfast each day, for instance, and within a week we're grabbing a toasted bacon sarnie as we run late into the office.

It's hard to break the habits of a lifetime . . . but it's not impossible! Now that you know you can lose unlovely flab when you have to for a special event—that holiday, wedding, major birthday party—why not try to keep those bulges at bay for the rest of your life?

You may see yourself as a podge who just CAN'T lose weight on a long-term basis. You tell yourself you have very little breakfast, a light lunch and only one main meal each day, so how come you put on weight? Perhaps it's in your genes or your metabolism?

Actually, it's almost certainly in your CALORIE-intake. All you need do is wise up on the calorie value of EVERYTHING you eat and drink.

It's no good just cutting down on food and hoping for the best. There are hidden calories lurking in everyday meals and nibbles which can bump up your daily intake to a staggering total.

For women, the big diet disaster areas are the sneaky snacks you enjoy at home or work—like biscuits with your tea, and cakes brought in because it's someone's birthday.

For men, that lunchtime pint is a killer when it's accompanied by high-calorie bar food. And even if you've cut out booze, your evening meal may be fat-loaded.

On the next page are two typical daily menus—for a man and woman in sit-down jobs. Neither is outrageously greedy—in fact, they probably think they eat very little!

And, with each menu we've worked out how the calories can be cut back—painlessly!

DAILY MENU ONE   For a woman, aged 25, working in an office.

Calorie needs: If she is simply trying to stay in shape, she needs just 2000 Calories daily (two thirds for body maintenance, the rest for activities). To lose weight, she must cut down to 1500 or less.

BREAKFAST	CALS
2 cups tea, a little milk, 1 tsp sugar in each	80
1 slice toast, 1/2 oz butter,	
2tsps marmalade	230
MID-MORNING	
1 cup coffee, milk, 1 tsp sugar	40
3 chocolate McVities Hob-Nobs	213
LUNCHTIME	
1 round ham salad sandwich	
with mayonnaise	400
1 apple	50
1 Mini swiss roll	145
AFTERNOON	
Cup of tea, milk, 1 tsp sugar	40
Mars Bar	295
SUPPER	
Medium helping Shepherd's Pie	300
Green beans with 1/2 oz knob of butter	105
2 tbs thick gravy	70
Fruit yogurt	140

NIGHTCAP
Drinking chocolate made with milk
and 1 tsp sugar   190
2 digestive biscuits   150
                            TOTAL: 2448

Unless she takes a LOT of exercise, this woman
will put ON weight at the rate of around 1lb a
week—which is about 3-1/2 stones a year!

She can save a massive 900 cals by: cutting out
sugar, butter, sweets and biscuits, taking a low-
calorie packed lunch to work (wholemeal sandwich, no butter or mayonnaise, fresh fruit), and
switching to lean meat or fish and lots of free veg
and salad for supper.

DAILY MENU TWO For a fella, age 30, also in an
office job. Calorie needs: just 2700 calories daily—
1700 if he wants to lose weight.

BREAKFAST	CALS
2 cups tea with milk, 2 tsps sugar	100
2 rounds toast, butter and marmalade	425
MID-MORNING	
2 cheese rolls	600
Yorkie Bar	320
Cup of coffee, milk, 2 tsps sugar	50

LUNCHTIME

2 pints lager	400
Cornish pasty	630
Pickled Egg	90
Packet of Crisps	125

MID-AFTERNOON

Cup of tea, milk, 2 tsps sugar	50
Jam doughnut	225

SUPPER

Large grilled pork chop	300
4 tbs mashed potatoes with 1 oz butter	360
4 tbs thick gravy	140
cabbage, carrots, peas	75
2 cups tea, milk, 2 tsps sugar	100
Apple pie and custard	450

NIGHTCAP

Cup of coffee, milk, 2 tsps sugar	50
2 digestive biscuits	150
TOTAL:	**4640**

Even though this fella is not a big boozer, he will soon be a big bulger. He is consuming almost DOUBLE the number of calories he needs. Cutting out sugar and butter will trim about 600 calories off the daily total. If he has a salad with his lunchtime pint (no dressing), and a low-fat evening meal, he'll shape up fast and have less chance of a heart attack later!

How those "own brand" foods shape up for fattening power...

Eating starts with shopping, which most of us do in supermarkets. Although many branded foods now have calorie details on the wrapper, some do not! And if you're bargain-hunting, the foods you choose are likely to be the ones without the info!

So, we've checked out the calorie content of some popular "own brand" foods from five top superstores. Take the list with you when you shop.

And, to help you plan your diet, we've included the values of the basic foods we eat every day.

To lose weight, women should trim their total daily intake back to about 1200 calories, and fellas should aim for around 1600. Make sure you vary the foods you eat—variety is the spice of life, and the secret of a healthy diet! And don't forget that fatty foods are bad for your heart and calorie-loaded—so cut down on baddies like butter, bangers and bathbuns!

BASIC FOODS:

	Calories
Bacon (1 back rasher, grilled)	50
Beef (6 oz grilled rump steak)	290
4 oz lean mince, fat drained	250
Bread (1 slice from wholemeal loaf)	70

Butter (1 tsp)	35
Cheese (1 oz Cheddar)	120
Chicken leg, skinned, grilled	170
Fruit (1 medium apple, orange, pear)	50
Fish (4 oz grilled, poached or steamed white fish—no fat)	120
Fresh green vegetables (large helping leafy greens, celery, cucumber etc)	neg.
Lamb (5 oz grilled chump chop)	200
Milk (1 pint silver top)	380
Milk (1 pint skimmed)	200
Pasta (4 oz boiled, any shape)	125
Sausages (large pork, grilled)	125
Tomatoes (1 medium)	8
Yogurt (5.3oz carton natural unsweetened)	100

DRINKS: Stick to water, mineral water, low-calorie soft drinks, and remember that there are 50 calories in each pub measure of spirits, and about 100 calories in a half pint beer or lager, or glass of dry wine.

SAINSBURY'S

BISCUITS (1 biscuit)

Digestive sweetmeal reduced sugar	45
Jaffa cake	45
Rich Tea finger cream	50

CEREALS (1oz, 25g portion)

Apricot wheats	95
Fruit and Fibre Flakes	103
Muesli	95
Wholewheat Bisk (2 Bisks)	120
High Fibre Bran	75

CAKES

Mini Swiss Rolls: 1 roll	125
Cherry Bakewell: 1 cake	185
Fruity Crisp	80

CANNED FRUIT (small can)

Blackberries in fruit juice	115
Pear halves in fruit juice	60
Fruit cocktail in juice	90

CANNED FISH (small can)

Sardines in Tomato Sauce	220

CANNED MEATS (small can)

Chicken in White Sauce	669
Chicken Breast in jelly	700
Chicken Curry	520
Minced Beef and Onion	350
Premium stewed steak	200

CANNED VEGETABLES (medium can)

Mushy peas	240
Curried beans	180
Chopped tomatoes with herbs	90

PIES

Crusty Bake Pork Pie (14 oz pie)	420

RECIPE DISHES (one pack)

Beef Stew with Dumpling	440
Chilli Con Carne	595
Lasagne	590
Vegetable Curry	285
Chicken Tikka Masala	320

SALAD SNACKS (one pack)

Prawn and Pasta	260
Coleslaw	255
Chicken Tikka	355

SOUPS (small can)

Chicken	190
Tomato	310
Minestrone	195
Oxtail	145
Mulligatawny	175
Spicy Lentil	140

SAFEWAY

CEREALS (1oz, 25g portion)

Cornflakes	107
Crunchy Cereal	118
Fibre Bran	70

BISCUITS (one biscuit)

All Butter Thin	25
Fruit shortcake	38

Milk Chocolate digestive	65
Milk Chocolate Orange Finger Wafer	50

CANNED FISH (medium can)

Pilchards in Brine	470
Tuna in curry sauce	300

CANNED FRUIT (small can)

Peach halves in natural juice	105
Fruit Cocktail in Syrup	215
Pineapple Rings in Natural Juice	115

CANNED VEGETABLES (small can)

Baked Beans	170
Garden Peas	140
Butter beans	85

CHILLED READY MEALS (one pack)

Chilli Con Carne	260
Seafood Lasagne	405
Sweet and Sour Pork with Rice	285
Vegetable Chilli	180

SANDWICHES (one sandwich)

Ham, Chicken and Salad	368
Corned Beef and Coleslaw	380
Egg Mayonnaise and Cress	387

SOUPS (medium can)

Tomato	210
Chicken	180
Mushroom	150

MARKS AND SPENCER—ST MICHAEL

BISCUITS (one biscuit)

Jaffa Cakes	45
Plain Chocolate Digestive	65
Brandy Snap	25
Chocolate Chip Cookies	60
Sultana Cookie	75

CAKES (one cake)

Fondant Fancies	110
Apple Slice	165
Raspberry Puff Slice	145

FROZEN PUDS

Black Currant Cheesecake (one slice)	185
Black Forest Gateau (1 gateau)	495
Baked Alaska	960
Lemon Torte	1010

MEAT DISHES (one pack)

Chilli Con Carne	2970
Chicken Jalfrezi	320
Chicken Risotto	350
Duckling a l'Orange	1110

VEGETABLE DISHES (one pack)

Vegetable Curry	180
Vegetable Chilli	395
Crispy Mushrooms	265
Vegetables in Lemon Herb Butter	235

SALADS (one pot)

Carrot and Nut	355
Florida Salad	460
Coleslaw	365
Lite Pasta and Salmon	175

SANDWICHES (one sandwich)

Bacon, lettuce and tomato	490
Prawn Mayonnaise (three-pack)	590
Roast Beef and Salad	265
Roast Chicken and Salad	400

ASDA

BISCUITS (one biscuit)

Almond Shortie, Lemon Crisp or Nice	45
Ginger Thin	25
Shortbread Finger	110
Fondant Fancy	95

CAKES

Cherry Bakewell	185
Milk Chocolate Roll	120

CHEESE (1oz, 25g)

Reduced Fat Soft Cheese	55
Roule Low Fat Herb and Garlic	44
Stilton with Apricots	104
Pineapple Cottage Cheese	24

CRISPS AND SNACKS

Bacon Bites (2oz, 50g)	230

Lower Fat Crisps, any flavour (1oz, 25g)	120
Prawn Cocktail Crisps (1oz, 25g)	125
Tortilla Chips (4oz, 100g)	455

FISH

Cod Steak in Breadcrumbs (100g)	185
Cod Steak in Mushroom sauce (100g)	155
Whole Plaice in Breadcrumbs (340g)	635

CANNED FRUIT

Fruit Cocktail in Juice (411g)	190
Mandarins in Juice (298g)	130
Prunes in Juice (220g)	175
Pears in Syrup (411g)	270

MEAT

Sweet and Sour Chicken Kiev (each)	250
Chicken Goujons (1oz)	64
Pork Bites with Cheese and Onion (each)	45

PUDDINGS

Chocolate sponge pudding (225g)	635
Creamed Rice Pudding (213g)	185
Black Forest Gateau (whole)	1870
Chocolate Mousse (62.5g)	125

CO-OP

BISCUITS (one biscuit)

Digestive Wheatmeal	70
Ginger Nut	40
Plain Chocolate Wheatmeal	80

CEREALS (1oz, 25g portion)

Cornflakes:	109
Choc chip muesli	114
Fruit with Fibre	107
Wholewheat cereal biscuits, each	65

CANNED VEGETABLES

Baked beans, reduced sugar and salt (439g)	325
Chilli beans (410g)	330

CANNED SOUPS (283g can)

Chicken	195
French Onion	80
Tomato	280

CANNED FRUITS IN JUICE (small can)

Apricot halves	160
Fruit cocktail	200
Pear halves	200

FISH AND MEAT (small can)

Minced Beef and Onions in gravy	315
Chicken in white wine	340
Sardines in tomato sauce	120
Pink salmon	140
Shepherd's pie (small frozen pie)	255

Great Drink-and-Slink Calorie Guide

Fancy a delicious, hot toddy, or a glass of bubbly? If you're trying to slim, too many little nips could give you big, wobbly hips!

For instance, did you know that a mug of hot chocolate, made with full-cream milk but without sugar "costs" around 150 Calories? That's the same as big plateful of chicken and salad with an apple to follow!

And, if you're reading this at breakfast, while knocking back that "healthy" orange juice, did you realise that a large glass contains 100 calories—the same as a half pint of lager?

To make absolutely sure that you're not kidding yourself about the hidden fattening power in drinks, here's a calorie guide to over one hundred favourites—from beer to Bovril:

	QUANTITY	CALS
Hot Toddies		
Bovril	1 tsp in water	10
Instant Bovril	1 sachet	20
Cadbury's Drinking		
Chocolate	2 tsps in water	40
	in 1/3 pt milk	150

Ovaltine Malted		
Drink	3 tsps in water	70
	in 1/3 pt milk	180
Oxo	1 level tsp in water	15
	1 cube chicken or beef	15
Lemon Tea	1 glass, no sugar	2

Fruit and Vegetable Juices

Britvic	113ml bottle,orange	
	or grapefruit	50
Campbells	1/4 pt tomato and veg	30
Del Monte	1/4 pt Apple	60
	1/4 pt orange	60
Just Juice	1/4 pt grapefruit	45
Libby's	1/4 pt Apple or	
	Pineapple "C"	65
	Orange "C"	55
PLJ	1 fl oz, all types	7
Sainsbury's	1/4 pt exotic fruit juice	55
St. Michael	1/4 pt freshly-squeezed	
	orange juice	20
	Lite Pineapple and	
	Passionfruit	25

Squashes

Boots Shapers	1 fl oz with water, all	
	flavours	2

Kia Ora	Low-cal Orange, 1 fl oz	
	with water	5
Ribena	Low sugar Light, 1 fl oz	
	undiluted	27
	250ml carton	50
Robinsons	Special 'R',	
	all flavours (1fl oz)	3
St. Clements	Orange squash, 1fl oz	
	with water	38

Mixers

Hunts	1/4 pt American Ginger ale	55
	1/4 pt tonic or lemonade	35
	1/4 pt low cal tonic	0
Schweppes	6.3fl oz bottle American	
	ginger ale	40
	Bitter Lemon	35
	Russchian, 500 ml	115
	Slimline, 6.3 fl oz bottle	0

Fizzy Drinks

Coca Cola	11.6oz can original	135
	Diet	0
Fanta	Orange Crush	
	11.6 oz can	120
Corona	1/4 pt ginger beer	40

Corona	Traditional Lemonade	55
	Low CalorieLemonade	1
Lucozade	250 ml bottle original	180
	Lucozade Light	45
Pepsi Cola	11.6fl oz can	145
	Diet	0

Vending Machines

Drinkmaster	Blackcurrant	35
	Coffee, white, no sugar	15
	Chocolate drink	70
	Chicken soup	40
	Orange drink	55
	Tea, white, no sugar	10
Maxpax	Blackcurrant	25
	Bovril	10
	Chocolate	65
	Lemon Tea	35
	Tomato Soup	20

Wine

Bordeaux Blanc	5 fl oz glass	100
Muscadet	"	95
Asti Spumante	"	120
Champagne	"	105
Mateus Rose	"	105
Beaujolais	"	100

Claret	5fl oz glass	95
Sweet White	"	125
Eisberg Alcohol free	"	35
Jung's Extra Dry white	"	10
Sainsbury's Low Alcohol	"	35
Masson Light	"	40

Beer

Courage Light	1/2 pt	75
Courage Best Bitter	"	100
John Smith's Bitter	"	95
Webster's Yorkshire	"	85
Guinness	"	100
Newcastle Brown Ale	"	110
McEwan's Export	"	105

Lager

Castlemaine XXXX	440 ml can	165
Lowenbrau	"	180
Carling Black Label	"	140
Skol	"	125
Lamot Pils	"	175
Hemeling	"	120
Foster's Draught	"	90
Hofmeister	"	80
Budweiser	"	110

Heineken	275ml can	85
Heldenbrau	440ml can	110
Heldenbrau Extra Special "		265
Coors Extra Gold	1/2 pint	115

Spirits
Whisky, gin, vodka, rum,bacardi, tequila, brandy,

bacardi	(pub measure, 25ml)	50
Jack Daniels	"	60
Southern Comfort	"	70

Liqueurs

Bailey's Original	"	80
Cadbury's Cream	"	75
Calvados	"	60
Creme de Menthe	"	80
Tia Maria	"	75

Aperitifs

Cinzano Extra Dry	Pub measure, 50ml	50
Dubonnet Dry	"	55
Martini Extra Dry	"	65
Campari	Pub measure, 25ml	55
Pernod	"	65

Sherry and Port

Tio Pepe	Pub Measure, 50ml	50
Croft Original	"	70
Harvey's Bristol Cream	"	85
Emva Cream	"	70
Tawny or Ruby port	"	75
Vintage port	"	80

Sally's Slimming Tips

Shape up with your favourite beach partner. Encourage each other to get into top form for that holiday of a lifetime. Stop going to the pub for lunch. Instead, meet up to go swimming or to the gym. Plan all the activities you'll enjoy on the trip. Spend hours poring over books about your destination. Plan long, candlelit dinners with low-calorie menus to get you in a holiday mood. Weigh in together every week: the one who shapes up best gets the new luggage, or outfit.

Eat regularly before you go. All our diet plans are carefully chosen to give you sustained nourishment throughout the day. If you miss meals, you'll wolf down mega-huge portions next time you eat. Even worse, you could gain loads of weight during your holiday. Ever noticed those holidaymaking hogs who gorge their way through all the nibbles and plastic meals on the holiday aircraft? They're the ones who tried to starve themselves for a few days before leaving home. It just doesn't work, folks!